READY TO WIN

READY TO WIN

HOW GREAT LEADERS SUCCEED THROUGH PREPARATION

MATTHEW MITCHELL

WINNING TOOLS

READY TO WIN
How Great Leaders Succeed through Preparation
First Edition

ISBN 979-8-9915542-0-6 *Hardcover*
      979-8-9915542-2-0 *Paperback*
      979-8-9915542-1-3 *Ebook*

This book is dedicated to my wife, Jenna Mitchell. Thank you for all of the love and effort you give to keep our family thriving. I love you!

CONTENTS

INTRODUCTION

In 1997, Michael Jordan made what would become a legendary television commercial for his Air Jordan brand. As the screen shows him stumbling on the court, turning the ball over, and missing shots, Jordan narrates:

> I've missed more than 9,000 shots in my career. I've lost almost 300 games. *Twenty-six times, I've been trusted to take the game-winning shot and missed.* I've failed over and over and over again in my life. And that is why I succeed.

At the very end, the commercial shows Jordan making one of his most famous game-winning shots to defeat the Utah Jazz for yet another NBA championship.

That is certainly an excellent message about overcoming failure, but I have a slightly different purpose in sharing it here. The middle of this quote that I've highlighted gets at something crucial—something essential to getting the most out of this book.

Let's take a quick step back so I can explain what I mean, and then come back to the Jordan quote and why it matters.

The title of this book makes the promise that it will get you *Ready To Win*. That raises a question, though: What exactly does it mean to you "to win?" Or, put another way: How do you measure and define success?

One way is to define success as short-term wins, and failure as temporary setbacks. Put that way, it sounds a little shallow—but if we are being honest, isn't it a very common (and very human) way to judge ourselves?

A sudden but temporary change in your industry's market conditions gives your revenue a brief spike. *Success!*

A big sale you thought was pretty much a done deal rapidly collapses and does not close. *Failure!*

We tend to ride the emotions of our latest triumph or disappointment and let them skew our judgment when we define our success.

Returning to the Jordan quote, this would be like judging his entire basketball career to be a failure by the 26 times he was trusted to take the game-winning shot and missed. Or, for that matter, calling it a success solely on the basis of one game-winning shot—even if that shot wins an NBA championship trophy.

Put in these terms, it is easy to see that judging a Hall of Fame career on any single play or game outcome would be ridiculous. What makes for a great career in sports or business is never a single outcome or result, or even a handful of them. What makes a Hall of Famer is sustained success.

That word *sustained* is absolutely key to understanding how I define the words "success" and "win" in this book. I am not interested in helping anyone get a temporary high or a one-off win. Real success should never be defined by short-term results.

Do not let your missed or made shots at the end of whatever game you are playing be your measuring stick. Instead, think of it this way: **True success is *sustained success*.**

That is the definition of winning that will allow you to get the most out of this book. It is also the definition of success that can make you a Hall of Fame-level leader in your chosen field.

I KNOW ALL ABOUT WINNING SHOTS THAT DO NOT FALL...

For 13 seasons, I was the head coach of the University of Kentucky women's basketball team. It was a terrific ride that included three visits to the Elite 8 of the NCAA tournament, a Southeastern Conference (SEC) championship, and three SEC Coach of the Year awards.

Of course, like any team, we learned all about game-winning shots that refuse to fall. It is just a part of basketball, and bound to happen. I had my share of other setbacks along the way: Super-talented recruits who chose to go elsewhere; a key hire that did not end up being the right fit; and one season where we had more losses than wins.

However, we only missed the NCAA tournament three times during my time there, and two of those misses were in my first two seasons. The program had sustained success for more than a decade.

The blueprint for this consistency was a set of principles I designed and committed to at the beginning of my collegiate head coaching career. In my previous book, *The Winning Tools*, I shared this set of three principles with business leaders.

The response to that book was gratifying. It received some tangible recognition by sparking invitations to deliver keynote speeches, requests for consulting engagements, and a spot on the *Wall Street Journal*'s bestseller list.

But that is all external stuff. I am a coach at heart—whether it be in basketball, business, or life—and what a coach always wants to do is make a real impact on lives. The outward signs of the book's success were nice, but what means more to me is that business leaders are implementing **The Winning Tools** in their careers and organizations and seeing results.

That book's success showed me it was time to go deeper and make more of an impact, and that has inspired this one. *Ready To Win* drills down into one of the most important skills that supports The Winning Tools: **Preparation.**

For those who have not read *The Winning Tools*, let me give you a quick orientation before explaining how Preparation fits in.

There are three Winning Tools: Honesty, Hard Work, and Discipline.

- **Honesty**: If you simply think of honesty as telling the bare minimum truth, then that's not a Winning Tool. The kind of honesty I'm talking about means surfacing all the issues, always acting with integrity, and being truthful with yourself about how much effort you're putting forth.

- **Hard Work**: To be a good leader, you need to help your team get a clear understanding of the value of hard work and how it can transform organizations (as well as lives). You also need to make sure that you and your team are working hard at the right things. People are willing to work harder once they understand its value.

- **Discipline**: The first two tools will lead you to the third. Discipline is the glue that will keep you honest and working hard. It is the consistency driven by discipline that powers long-term success.

I will refer to these three fundamentals often as a way to show how great leaders prepare their teams to win. Even though world-class Preparation involves all three tools, it has a special connection to Hard Work.

Each Winning Tool has three pillars that support them. The three pillars of Hard Work are Preparation, Sacrifice, and Resilience.

I will not say that Preparation is necessarily more important than the other pillars, but I can say this: If you fail to work hard and think hard during preparation, no amount of talent or performance under pressure is going to save you.

This is something so simple and easy to understand, but yet it is a failure I see over and over in sports, business, and life. I will give you a very basic example from basketball.

Let's say it is nearing the end of a college basketball season and a team is gearing up to play a tough conference game in late February. The coach has watched enough video to design a game plan that exploits the weakness of the opponent. The plan will rely on lots of full-court press and pressure defense.

The coach has correctly identified the perfect plan in terms of strategy—the upcoming opponent is definitely weak in handling pressure for a full game.

However, there is a big problem. The coach's own team is not physically capable of sustaining the strategy. Compared to the rest of the world, the athletes are no doubt in good physical shape. But they are not in good enough shape to apply the relentless pressure that would likely win them the game.

Another way to put it: This upcoming game was lost the previous summer when the team's pre-season conditioning was not taken seriously enough. In many instances in sports and business, a lack of preparation simply cannot be made up for.

How many businesses struggle with this same concept? Let's say you are a leader in a company that relies on a complex sales process with a long cycle. What your team is doing right now to make initial contact with prospects will directly impact whether you will meet your sales goal several months or even a year from now. You may be already losing that "game" right now, and nothing your team does later can make up for it.

There is another huge problem for leaders who fail to get their teams ready to win: You are guaranteed to lose the confidence of your team. People do not like to lose, but what's even worse is feeling like you are in a no-win position.

If you do not get your team ready to succeed, confidence erodes. Eventually, if it happens enough times, you will be a leader in name only (and maybe not even in name if you lose your position because of it).

You might think you are winning friends and earning trust with your team by being easy with them about accountability and preparation, but what you are actually doing is setting yourself up to let them down.

As a leader, you show your team exactly how much you care about them when you place a premium on accountability and preparation. Great leaders are honest enough to consistently hold people accountable for the process and habits of preparation.

For those who are not yet in a leadership position but striving for one, you will also greatly benefit from what you learn here. Nothing makes someone stand out as promotable as much as someone who is consistently prepared and confident.

A ROADMAP FOR SUCCEEDING THROUGH PREPARATION

At a high level, here is how this journey to great preparation will go. It is broken into two parts. The first part is all about the mindsets you need to be a leader of great preparation. These are the "thinking filters" great leaders need to both model and instill in others.

The early chapters will clearly define and explain these three foundational mindsets that grow a person of sustained success:

- **Excellence is Its Own Reward**
- **Belief in Sustained Success**
- **Commitment to Constant Preparation**

My goal for changing mindsets goes beyond just defining and explaining them. I certainly want to do that, but **I also want to give you daily exercises that will make them stick.** Getting initially excited about changing your mindset is relatively easy, but truly changing at a deep level is harder.

The daily mindset exercises can make this transformation happen if you commit to them and continue them even when you are feeling low or facing adversity. In fact, you will especially need these daily practices when you hit a rough patch. You will find daily exercises in the final chapter of this book.

Understanding mindsets is the critical foundation of a leader who is always ready to win. However, you have to build on that foundation with practical steps. The second half of this book walks you through a proven three-step way to achieve championship-level preparation.

☐ Step 1: Get crystal clear on your goal(s).
☐ Step 2: Create a strategy for how you will prepare to meet those goal(s).
☐ Step 3: Execute the details of that strategy with maximum effort and accountability.

This third step is itself broken into two parts: How you as a leader personally go through your own preparation, and then how you guide your team through excellent preparation.

SEPARATING YOURSELF AS A LEADER

Why do some business leaders become wildly successful, while others seem to get stuck grinding out mediocre careers?

If consistently practiced, The Winning Tools will create first-class leaders and separate them from those who cannot make the leap. To take it one step further and deeper, mastering Preparation will amplify all the benefits that come from the framework of Honesty, Hard Work, and Discipline.

Once you have internalized the mindsets and then mastered the three steps of Preparation (goal, strategy, and execution), you will have the key to separating yourself as a person who can handle tremendous responsibility and earn the financial rewards that come along with it.

To put it another way: You will not have to hunt for sustained success.

It will find you.

HOW DO GREAT LEADERS THINK ABOUT PREPARATION?

T WAS MY FIRST YEAR AS A HEAD COACH AT KENTUCKY, and we were on our way to the University of Georgia for a tough conference road game.

The season to date had been up and down, but this team had demonstrated they had the talent to be competitive—even against challenging opponents. The calendar was about to flip to February, and we were deep into Southeastern Conference (SEC) matchups. It is in conference play that a team's season is ultimately judged a success or failure.

Even though it was my first year, my vision for the program was to become a consistent powerhouse within the SEC, and sooner rather than later.

I knew this road game at Georgia was the kind of matchup we would need to start winning at least some of the time if we wanted to be considered a top program in the SEC. Their Hall of Fame Coach Andy Landers had led Georgia to decades of excellence, including several Final Four appearances and SEC championships.

In short: If you want to be a consistent powerhouse, you have to start beating other powerhouses.

The day of the game, we had a practice and I told my players, "We are going to be ahead at the end of this game, and we are going to need to stop them to finish off the game."

Of course, I could not be sure of that, but I knew we had the talent and toughness to match Georgia blow for blow—even on the road. By saying this to the team, I wanted to inject some belief and confidence that this was a game we could win. I also wanted to emphasize that when we find ourselves in a position to win, we need to be the kind of team that finishes games.

Telling them that was "talking the talk," though; I wanted to give them something that would help them "walk the walk." In short, I wanted to give them the practical substance of excellent preparation.

From film scouting, I knew Georgia was likely to run a flair screen in a particular way if they needed a 3-point basket in a crucial situation. It can be a difficult play to defend—especially near the end of the game, when pressure sometimes makes players forget where they are supposed to be defensively.

So, in practice that day, we walked through how we would defend it.

Sure enough, the game was tied 44–44 as the clock went under 30 seconds. We had possession, and called timeout and designed a play to get us an open look on the left wing from 3-point range. It worked to perfection and guard Samantha Mahoney nailed the shot.

Now the exact situation we had prepared for in practice was here. Georgia would need to make a 3-point shot to send the game into overtime. Because we were prepared for this play, it was almost as if Georgia passed it directly to our guard, Lydia Watkins. She did exactly what we'd practiced, secured the steal, dribbled out the clock, and we had a big road win.

I should add that it was perfect that Lydia was the one who secured the win. Lydia played about 12 minutes a game and was a great "team-first" player. Her stat lines were not flashy, but she did the little things that often go overlooked. On that night, she earned the thrill of securing the win, and it was well-deserved.

A great deal of confidence came from that win, and we went on to take a giant leap forward. Of course, that leap forward was not just about any one play. It also could have easily come down to some other shot or play that decided the game—perhaps one that we had not anticipated or did not execute as well.

That night in Georgia, however, we *were* prepared for that play, and it energized our team. As a first-year coach in the SEC, it also gave me a boost of confidence. Seeing what preparation could do also fired up the players' enthusiasm for more of it throughout the season. Success breeds success. Confidence breeds more confidence.

My team had learned a valuable lesson: **Preparation powerfully positions you to win more often.**

There is an old saying about casinos that "the house always wins." Strictly speaking, that is not true on any given bet or game, but it is true that they have set up the percentages and odds in such a way that overall, they will always make a profit.

Preparation makes you "the house," although perhaps in a more fair way! If you powerfully position yourself to win again and again, you will win more times than you lose.

Those wins accumulate, and the benefits for you and those you lead will grow exponentially. While a well-prepared leader and his team may lose individual battles, looking at the big picture, a consistently prepared leader literally cannot lose.

If preparation is that important, why are so many people not that great at it? Some of this is because people do not understand the mindsets and processes of first-class preparation. It also has to do with a lack of commitment to the task of preparation.

To start getting a grasp on this subject, I am going to walk you through the five different levels of competence in preparation. In my experience, everyone falls into one of these categories. As you read through each level, I recommend thinking about what your current level is. Use the first Winning Tool of Honesty, and sincerely ask yourself which category best describes you.

THE 5 PREPARATION LEVELS

The five "Cs" that define levels of preparation are:

- Casual
- Cursory
- Compliant
- Committed
- Constant

Casual

This lowest level of preparation is random, with little to no intent or thought behind it. To put it in familiar terms, this is often known as "winging it."

Most readers are unlikely to fall into this category. Just the fact that you have a book on preparation in your hands shows an intention and an interest—something casual preparers do not have.

However, it can happen that we slip up on this in some important tasks or areas of our lives. You get hyper-focused on one part of your job or life and the preparation is good to great. But then you fall down and become very random in other areas.

This can happen when you have a few particular tasks at work you dread, and you show it by being chronically unprepared to face those situations.

Or maybe you have areas involving your personal health or relationships that you consistently do not address because you are so focused on your career. Eventually, your lack of planning and preparation on key personal issues will begin distracting you and nagging at your peace of mind. This hurts your overall ability to be a consistent performer.

I am not saying you need a 10-point battle plan for every aspect of your life or career, but you do need to think carefully about where your preparation may be lacking.

The Results You Can Expect at the Casual Level of Preparation: *Lighting Strike.* In other words, random preparation = random results.

Reflection Question for the Casual Level: *Are there areas of my life that are hurting my overall success because I am ignoring preparation?*

Cursory

This is a slight step up from Casual, but it is still an exceptionally shallow and brief kind of preparation. When you are

Cursory, you do more than just wing it, but if you look closely, the substance and completeness is lacking.

Think of it like that time back when you were in school and forgot to do your homework. You scribbled down some answers as you rode the bus and hoped the teacher wouldn't look too closely and see the poor quality of your work or discover that you skipped a few questions.

Anyone at this level of preparation is essentially just looking to stay out of trouble or avoid the embarrassment of not being prepared at all. Of course, the irony is that a person looks even more foolish if they get called out for sloppy, shallow preparation.

Again, my assumption is that most readers of this book already do better than this in most key areas of your life. However, if you are struggling at the Cursory level, keep reading. If you commit to taking action based on what you learn, you can advance a couple levels by committing to new ways.

The Results You Can Expect at the Cursory Level of Preparation: *Hit or Miss.* If you happen to prepare for the right things, you might occasionally score a "hit," but more often it will be a "miss."

Reflection Question for the Cursory Level: *Think of a few times in your life when you really felt the sting of not being prepared. Why do you think it happened?*

Compliant

This is a level of preparation where you pretty much do what is expected and no more.

If you are at this level, you are driven by external expectations rather than an inner drive (at least when it comes to preparation). In other words, you are complying, but you are not going any extra steps.

I call this a "check-the-box" mentality, and it can be easy to slip into this mode and then stay there for an entire mediocre career. That may sound a little harsh, but this happens all the time. A person can spend a career staying busy working on inessential things. These folks can never seem to find enough time to prepare in a way that powerfully positions them to win.

Let me give you an example from our scouting reports when I was at Kentucky. During my time there, I would rotate the assignment from game to game as to who was in charge of the report.

Through the years, I would notice some assistants treating it as something to just churn out because it was asked of them. The thought behind it seemed to be: "This is a work product. It was my job to produce it. I did it."

Don't get me wrong, it was better than cursory work—but it had no drive behind it, no searching curiosity, and no stretching to find an extra gear. It had almost the flavor of, "Look teacher, I did my homework, and I did it well enough."

The compiling of these kinds of compliant scouting reports often consisted of calling a buddy in the coaching network and saying, "Hey, what do you have on Florida [or whatever school they were scouting]?"

That would have been a good place to start, but for some that was pretty much where it ended. Again, it was not that the report was wrong, but rather that it had a flavor of cut and paste, of something mechanical.

It reminds me of some head coaches who learn how to structure practices from a great coach they have worked for previously. Then, they copy it exactly and consider it "good to go." In one sense, there is nothing wrong with this approach. We should learn from mentors. Thank goodness I worked for so many great coaches and was able to take ideas and structure from all them.

However, you also have to make things your own, and you are always going to have to make adjustments that make sense for your team. The Compliant level cannot get you there.

The surest sign of being at the Compliant level of Preparation is that box-checking mentality I mentioned above. You do everything you are supposed to, but without digging any deeper. "All the boxes are checked, I did the job."

Another quality of the Compliant mentality is to do the preparation, consider it finished, and then sit back and wait for the rewards to roll in. Seasoned, mature leaders recognize that preparation does not guarantee you will always win, and never expect that they are entitled to kick back and wait for the wins and accolades to fall all over them. This is especially true if only average, box-checking preparation has been completed.

The Results You Can Expect at the Compliant Level of Preparation: *Average*. When you prepare at an average level, you cannot expect more than average results.

Reflection Questions for the Compliant Level: *Am I a box-checker, or do I look to go deeper in my preparation? Do I look to others to hand me success for doing a respectable job, or do I think my success is ultimately up to me?*

Committed

This is where you put the box-checking mentality in the rear view mirror and start proactively taking responsibility for your preparation. The energy you are devoting to this comes from an internal drive to be a person of integrity and substance.

You are proactively taking responsibility for the preparation and not just looking at it as a work product to please the boss or some other authority.

Continuing the example of a scouting report, you take it to another level. You ask yourself: "Given what I have put together about the other team's tendencies and tactics, what are some practical and strategic ways I can take this knowledge and use it to help us win the game?"

At this level, you also maturely accept that being ready to win does not mean you will win every time (recall Michael Jordan missing those 26 game-winning shots). You should of course learn from any failures that happen because of mistakes in preparation—but as for the rest, you do not dwell on anything outside of your control.

At this commitment level, you will start to get a taste of what it is like to inhabit a world of excellence (an important concept that we will dive into extensively in Chapter 2). You will be on the road to sustained success.

The Results You Can Expect at the Committed Level of Preparation: *Productive and Profitable.* When you commit to preparation excellence, you are going to get a boost of confidence in pressure situations. You will still make mistakes, and you will not always know what you don't know, but you will start to notice your wins increasing.

Reflection Questions for the Committed Level: *Does the word "committed" describe how prepared I am for important career and personal situations? Would those that I lead (or work for) describe me as committed to preparation?*

Constant

In my experience, you cannot get to this highest level without two things: Time and guidance. You cannot instantly will yourself to reach this masterful level of preparation just by deciding to do it. You can choose to be at the Committed level, but joining this top level will take time and learning from other leaders who are master preparers.

In my own case, the leader who opened me up to a relentless pursuit of excellent preparation was Mickie DeMoss. I was an assistant at Kentucky for Coach DeMoss for two seasons (this was before becoming the head coach a couple of years later).

At that time, I had been at the collegiate level as an assistant coach for four years. Long enough to be decent at it, but still have a whole lot to learn. One thing I had in my favor was that I was motivated, and I was definitely not looking to just check boxes. In short, I was at the Committed level of preparation.

So, into her office I would go with my scouting report for our next opponent. I began going through particular plays and sharing what I thought was a pretty complete breakdown. After going through a play and giving my thoughts on what we could do to have our team be ready for it, Coach DeMoss would often have a question for me.

"And what do they do after that?"

Or, she would ask, "What happens when they run this kind of play instead of the one you just described?"

I'd respond, "I don't know, I haven't seen that."

And she would reply, "Well, go find out."

She exposed me to a certain kind of relentlessness in preparation. A willingness to ask the next question, and the one after that; to be prepared for one level, and then peel that back and go several layers deeper.

If you want to go from Committed to the mastery level of Constant preparation, a good path to follow is seeking out leaders who model it themselves. The more you can be around transformational preparers like Coach DeMoss, the more you will truly understand what a dedicated, "no stone unturned" philosophy looks like.

Of course, you will observe their specific habits and best practices—but on an even deeper level, through something almost like osmosis, the mindsets of transformational preparers will also rub off on you.

You'll see the kind of success they generate, the kind of person they are, and you'll want to follow them. They are unmistakably leaders because they refuse to let anyone outwork or out-prepare them.

In my own career, I ask myself what would have happened to me if I had never worked for Coach DeMoss. Would I have even known there was another level? Part of this book's goal is to make sure every reader is exposed to this extra, sometimes hidden level of preparation that great leaders attain.

In the same way, I often wonder what would have happened if I had not learned from Billy Donovan. He has been an excellent NBA coach since 2015—and before that he had tremendous success at University of Florida, including back to back national championships. My time as an assistant for

Florida's women's team overlapped with Coach Donovan's time there, and we struck up a friendship.

In observing Coach Donovan, I can tell you his success is no accident. He is one of the most detail-oriented leaders you could ever meet. It was my exposure to him and his detailed preparation and practices that helped me see what sustained success looks like in real life.

The other ingredient for going from Committed to Constant is time. In many ways, preparation is a skill you learn, and there will always be nuances in your particular profession or craft. Whether it is sales, marketing, coaching, executive leadership, or anything else, you will learn where you need to go deeper in your preparation if you are committed to it. You cannot know what you do not know until you have enough experience.

That is absolutely fine. Stay committed and your development will happen. Remember, too, that greatness also consists in knowing this: Growth should never stop. If you are looking to get to that mythical place where you know everything and non-stop success will just come to you, then you can forget about it right now, because there is no such thing. True preparation experts never stop pushing themselves to become better and expand their knowledge. It is how they became masterful preparers in the first place.

It's amazing what you can do for yourself both professionally and personally when you are a master of preparation. You separate yourself in a way that gives you confidence and sustained success, where those who came unprepared will realize they have been beaten before they've even gotten started.

The Results You Can Expect at the Constant Level of Preparation: *Sustained Success.* Think of the most successful coaches and business leaders. Was there any chance that Warren Buffet wasn't going to be successful at whatever he chose to do? Would Pat Summit or John Wooden have failed anywhere? No chance, because they did not leave it up to chance. Focused, constant preparers achieve sustained success. Think of this, too. You do not have to achieve those astronomical heights to enjoy an amazing life filled with sustained success and life-changing impact on others. It is all there for you. Commit to excellent preparation, and then let time and experience do their thing. It works every time.

Reflection Questions for the Constant Level: *How can you connect with leaders who are master preparers? Are you showing the kind of hard work in preparation that makes leaders want to invest time in you?*

My assumption if you are reading this book is that you *do* want to be excellent at preparation. No one ever says, "My plan is to stay mired in procrastination and bad preparation habits."

Yet, some people cannot seem to break through and stay committed to preparation for the long haul. Why?

PREPARATION KILLERS

Let's identify and discuss the three main blocks to becoming a master preparer:

- Self-sabotage
- Lack of clarity
- Fear of pressure

Let's look at each one in turn.

Self-Sabotage Inside Your Own Head

Young, immature leaders tend to put too much emphasis on specific outcomes, but not enough on the preparation steps it takes to achieve that result.

Of course, you do want to have clarity around the outcomes and goals (as we are about to discuss further below). However, once you have that clarity, the day-to-day focus should be on the process and preparation that drives the result you want, not the result itself.

When you put too much emphasis on the outcome and not enough on the process of preparation, you realize you are not ready to win (and it begins to dawn on your team, too). Negative mindsets begin to create a downward spiral. Essentially, bad mindsets are a form of self-sabotage because they are not true, but they also keep you from seeing the way out.

That is why the next three chapters will give you the mindsets that crush self-sabotage and keep you driving your team in the direction of sustained success.

Lack of Clarity

Problems around clarity tend to impact leaders at all levels of experience.

New leaders are trying to get their arms around the skills they need to succeed. They may also be inexperienced at setting goals that reliably predict success.

On the other hand, experienced leaders who produce sustained success tend to be the people that get promoted. The further they climb, the bigger their responsibilities and the more people they are responsible for guiding. This increases complexity, and complexity often kills clarity.

Chapter 5 will dive deep into details about clarity and goals—but for now, let me just make a more general point here that can be helpful.

Whether you are a new leader wrestling with problems you have never faced before or a seasoned veteran suddenly faced with complexity, remember: Clarity comes to leaders who can stay calm under all circumstances. It allows you to recall your fundamental principles, even in a crisis.

Well into my tenure at Kentucky, I hired an assistant who did not end up being a good fit for the program. Because I was too slow to see it, this ended up creating a big player exodus and bad feelings. At first, I dove headfirst into the crisis, just trying to fight brush fires every day. This mentality was taking up all my energy and pushing aside process-oriented preparation and steady leadership. I was getting lost in complexity, chaos, and piecemeal thinking.

At a certain point, I realized this was not working, and to get clarity I had to go back to my principles: The Winning Tools. For every problem I ran into, I started asking which bucket to put it into.

- Was this a problem Honesty could solve?
- Was this a problem Hard Work could solve?
- Was this a problem Discipline could solve?

It still wasn't an easy time, but this principle-centered approach allowed me to cut through temporary solutions and see with a clarity that allowed genuine progress toward actual solutions.

Turning Away from Pressure

It is human nature to not want to look like a fool. And it is human nature to not want to lose.

When we know we are going to have to go into the arena—whether it be a game, a sales call, or a presentation for investors—we know we might end up losing. We might even end up looking foolish.

Theoretically, this should make us prepare harder—but instead it often makes us procrastinate. We procrastinate because preparing to go into the arena reminds us of the pressure we are going to face. And because we do not want to look foolish or lose, we turn away from that pressure and go do some "busy work" task that takes our mind off of what we really need to be doing.

If procrastination and an underlying fear of pressure are a problem for you, the next three chapters on mindset will help. You will learn that there is a cure, and it is a combination of well-trained habits of mind combined with a focus on process over outcome.

You can actually get a tremendous amount of relief from that terrible feeling of being an unprepared procrastinator if you are willing to work on your mindsets and commit to the process. This is not a magic pill; it is a realistic re-framing of how you prepare, and it will make you more productive than you thought possible.

DO YOU WANT THE KIND OF TEAM THAT CAN CLOSE OUT A GAME?

In the NFL, one of the key measures of quarterback greatness is game-winning drives. It is not too much to say that the ability to lead your team down the field with the game on the line can be the difference between a somewhat average career and the Hall of Fame.

The top 5 list of all-time game-winning drives tells the story: Tom Brady, Peyton Manning, Drew Brees, Ben Roethlisberger, and Dan Marino. Manning and Marino are already in the Hall of Fame, and the other three are locks to get in as soon as they are eligible. It is no accident that they have 12 Super Bowl rings in total.

PEYTON MANNING ON PREPARATION

It is my excellent good fortune to call Hall of Fame quarterback Peyton Manning a friend. Peyton earned a reputation for exceptional preparation during the course of his football career, which included two Super Bowl championships. I asked if he would be willing to answer a few questions about the topic of preparation, and he generously agreed.

1. You gained a reputation for your relentless preparation during your time in the NFL. Where did that passion for preparation come from? Were there "light bulb" moments along the way that made you become even more passionate about preparation?

"I've always been a big believer in work ethic and preparation. All competitors are looking for an edge, and I thought mine could come through preparation. I knew I wasn't going to be able to outrun defenders or throw the ball 80 yards down the field, but preparing harder and working harder gave me confidence that I could find my advantage.

"One light bulb moment happened when I got to the University of Tennessee and I realized just how much film you could study at that level. In high school there is just not a lot of video available to watch. Then you get to the college level and you realize how much is available, that there is just so much film you can study. You can watch video of your opponents, of course, but I could also watch every play from last year that our offense ran, and every play in our spring practice and so on. There is enough that you can always be studying and taking notes and improving all the time.

"Another light bulb moment is that mistakes can actually give you confidence if you make them in practice and then study them. You practice, and then you watch the film of the practice and write down the positives and the negatives. You use that the next day to get better and correct mistakes. At Tennessee, I learned to get really confident with particular plays and then when it is time for kick off on Saturday, you feel good and ready to execute.

"Make your mistakes, figure out what went wrong, and make improvements. You do this until you have a level of confidence that allows you to execute in games."

2. How about preparation in the NFL? You were known for game-winning drives, and I would think preparation had a lot to do with that.

"As far as preparation for NFL late game drives, one key was to create game time conditions during the week of practice. During the two-minute drill, we had the scoreboard rolling with the game clock going and we had speakers piping in loud crowd noise. Nothing can quite simulate a live stadium crowd, but the noise was still right on top of you from the speakers.

"Another way it was like a game was that you wanted to win even though you were driving against your own defense. When the offense was stopped, the defense celebrated and all of us on offense were disappointed. That disappointment makes you go back and watch what happened and figure out why we didn't score. Then you correct it at the next practice. This is similar to what I was saying about my college experience. It builds confidence when you figure out where you failed to execute and then you improve it. You keep working to get it right and improve the execution.

"The overall point is that you want a Thursday practice to feel like a Sunday game. When you treat practice and preparation like a real game, you are ready. Those game-like conditions—the crowd noise, our defense playing the opponent's scheme, the game clock, all of it—gives you confidence in the final minutes of a game on Sunday. When you line up, you have already seen it and you feel prepared. It allows you to thrive in the moment and not be overwhelmed by it."

3. You have been very active in your post-NFL career in many different areas, including business, entertainment, and philanthropy. How have your world-class football preparation skills carried over into success in those areas?

"Preparation serves you well in any field. I think two big things for me that have carried over are asking questions and note taking.

"I always liked to ask questions. It is one of the preparation skills that I learned playing football and it still applies for me today. Whether it's a charity project or a business project or whatever it is, I try to ask questions that help me understand what needs to be done and why we are doing it. Otherwise, you are going to end up in an uncomfortable spot or be caught off guard.

"The other thing is that I am still a note taker. I did it in football, and I still do it. I believe writing things down gets them ingrained into your brain in a deeper way. It is something that has continued to serve me well."

I took several insights from Peyton's answers that everyone can implement in their own preparation:

One, when you get access to more preparation resources, use them! Peyton instantly recognized that the amount of film available in college compared to high school was extraordinary. He took full advantage of that.

Two, the more you can make your preparation match actual conditions, the more you can let your mistakes happen during practice. This can drive up your confidence as you learn and see improvement. This seems like especially valuable advice for any kind of preparation for speaking or presenting.

Three, asking questions and note taking are ways to deepen your understanding and preparation. Building these habits will serve anyone well.

This special ability to close out games is directly tied to hard work and preparation. After a time, a team begins to believe in its quarterback leader when the game is on the line. They have the confidence that they will close out the game with a win. It will not happen every time, but it will many more times than not.

At the beginning of this chapter, I shared how the 2008 Kentucky team sealed a tough victory on the road against

Georgia—a win which gave us confidence that we could compete with any team in the SEC and win more times than not.

It would take another season before we became a program that almost never missed the NCAA tournament and would often advance deep, but the seeds of belief had been planted. My players became convinced that a big part of our team identity was that we could close out games. When new players came in, they were schooled in this same culture by the older players.

Then the new players became the older players, and the cycle of belief continued. It was our commitment to preparation that fueled our ability to close out games. Then we would win, and that belief got ingrained, which in turn spurred all of us to be more passionate about preparation.

That is the kind of cycle that drives sustained success. If you want that in your own career and on your team, it all starts with three mindsets.

MINDSET #1:
EXCELLENCE IS ITS OWN REWARD

M AKAYLA EPPS IS ONE OF THE BEST PLAYERS THAT I ever coached—just a great, great basketball player. She has talent to burn, a charisma that makes her stand out, and an energy that feeds off of crowds and excitement.

But in the late spring of 2015 at the end of her sophomore year, we had a problem. Makayla called me late one afternoon and said, "Coach, I need to tell you something. A few weeks ago, I was arrested for underaged drinking and having an open container of alcohol."

When I heard this, I wasn't particularly upset. When you work with young people day in and day out, they will inevitably make mistakes. The "a few weeks ago" comment did bother me a bit, and I was curious why she was telling me now instead of immediately after it had happened.

I got my answer to that question when I hung up the phone. My assistant coach came to me and said, "Coach, you need to check the Lexington Herald-Leader website." There on the site was a flashing red alert: "BREAKING NEWS: UK Women's basketball star *arrested!*"

I suddenly understood why Makayla was telling me now. The news of the incident was now public, and it was inevitable that I would find out. Unfortunately for her, she had received advice not to tell me before. She was advised that the situation would be "handled behind the scenes" and it was nothing I "needed to know."

At the time, our program had found its way into the spotlight because our teams had done well for years (and also, this is Kentucky, where basketball is near religion). It got worse the next morning when the story found its way to the front page of the print edition! Suddenly what was a pretty typical mistake from a college-aged student became big news. It was understandable because Makayla was regarded as one of the best basketball players in the country on one of the best teams.

More than the incident itself, what bothered me most was that Makayla did not tell me what happened until after it had already blown up. I always emphasized with my players that we were responsible for our actions and that our actions reflected on our individual character and reputation.

We also were the most visible group of female athletes in the state of Kentucky, and thousands of people looked up to us and were inspired by what we'd accomplished on the court. We took our responsibility as role models seriously, and we stressed to the entire organization that our character and actions reflected not just on us, but the whole team.

I was caught flat-footed when I was called by the media, and I told Makayla, "Listen, we cannot operate this way, with you not telling me things. You have a big responsibility to yourself, your teammates, and to the overall program."

I felt that some extra discipline was warranted, so she was suspended from the team for a time—and that included missing the popular "Big Blue Madness" fan rally to kick off the season. She really loved the energy of that night, so I knew this would be especially hard on her.

What I did was sit her down and lay out an agreement in front of her. I said: "*Either you are going to sign on to this agreement and fulfill it and come back to the team, or you can transfer somewhere. There are plenty of people out there who will welcome you and use you for your basketball talent, and they won't care about any of this or help you grow as a person. It is your decision.*"

Think about this for a minute from Makayla's perspective. Here is a young person—not even 20 years old yet. All the time she was growing up, she was no doubt the best player on the court by a wide margin. On top of that, everyone was surely always complimenting her on how great she was, and then on top of that, her natural charisma made her a popular person. She was easily one of the three most popular players to ever play at Kentucky during my 15 seasons associated with the program.

In addition, like I said, she would not have a problem finding takers if she wanted to transfer.

In short, she had every reason to keep going on her talent and charm, and reject the discipline. Many nineteen year olds would have done exactly that.

To her great credit, she signed the discipline agreement, and then fulfilled it to the letter. She got back with the team and had two more outstanding seasons. In fact, she showed tremendous grit and determination in her senior year, when I went through my toughest year as a coach and we were down to six scholarship players.

She carried us on her back—now with not just the talent, but great character, too. We still made the NCAA tournament that year, and we also beat the #2 team in the country on her senior night.

The discipline agreement gave her two possible directions: She could have said, "The heck with Coach Mitchell and the heck with the program," and just gone somewhere else. Or, she could say, "I did not live up to the standard, I am going to accept it, pay the price, and get back with my team."

To put it in the simplest terms possible: When faced with a choice, Makayla chose to inhabit a world of excellence.

Hold that thought for a moment, because I want to take a few steps back and talk about what mindsets are and how they can help anyone become a person of character and preparation.

WHAT ARE MINDSETS, REALLY?

At the most fundamental level, **mindsets are the habits we use when thinking about and processing our lives.** They are the habits we have ingrained in our brains.

To give a super-simple example, we all know people with "Chicken Little" personalities where the sky is always falling. Essentially, they have built a habit of mind that interprets almost everything as a sign that things are falling apart.

We could probably identify dozens of other mindsets (good and bad) and name them. However, I think time is better spent focusing on the ones that work—the mindsets that will give you the foundation to be always ready to win.

Once you understand the right mindsets, you have to actively and consciously *choose* those mindsets. People who get fixed in certain unhealthy mindsets miss this incredibly crucial fact: We are not stuck permanently with our mindsets. We can choose our mindsets, and we should choose them with great intention.

I do not deny that how we are raised and other life experiences will have an impact on the habits of our mind. Depending on how we were guided, that can be good or bad (or some mixture of the two). However, that does not mean we cannot change the bad habits of mind and reinforce the good ones.

Here is what I am asking you to do. Read through this and the next two chapters. Take in the information on these mindsets, and get a good grasp of them.

At that point, you will be in a position to actively *choose* these mindsets or not. One thing I cannot do is make the choice for you. This is often the key missing ingredient in self-development books. They often fail to emphasize that it takes an active choice to say "I am going to change my brain habits," and that has to come first.

It is your choice, and no book or seminar or business coach or anyone else can actively choose it for you.

Please do not misunderstand what I am saying. I am not claiming that just by saying you choose a new mindset, that change will be accomplished instantly. It will take consistently using the mindset exercises over time to shift your thinking. It will mean digging a little deeper when you face some adversity and not falling back into the same thought patterns.

But it starts with the choice, and everything can change when you make that choice and then sincerely commit to backing it up with daily exercises (which will be shared in Chapter 9).

Key Point: Mindsets are habits of mind, and habits are choices you make consistently. Therefore, it logically follows that you can choose your mindset and then reinforce it with action.

Let's return now to the first of the foundational mindsets of a prepared leader. A great leader understands that Excellence is Its Own Reward.

There are three key beliefs that those leaders with an "Excellence is Its Own Reward" mindset share:

- They believe that all their actions matter, whether big or small.
- They know that rewards are a byproduct of a life well-lived.
- They get great satisfaction from inhabiting a "world of excellence."

Stick with this for a few more paragraphs, because it is important to grasp the underlying theme here. We will soon tie this back to why this matters for preparation.

All Actions Matter

I am reminded of our local grocery store growing up, Vowell's Sunflower. After you'd loaded your groceries into the car, you had the choice of just leaving the cart free-floating there in the parking lot or going back to the store and returning the cart.

My dad always insisted that the cart be walked back to the store. I remember grumbling a little bit about this in my head. What did it matter? I even recall that one of my brothers, Mark, worked at the store, and it was one of his jobs to gather up carts and bring them back. So, even the grocery store did not expect you to bring the cart back because they had hired people to do it!

However, I now see it differently. What my dad was doing was teaching me "the how" of living in a world of excellence. "The how" is all about *not* cutting corners, even when it is a small thing that is easy to excuse as being unimportant.

The reasoning was as simple as it was excellent: You use the cart, you return it where you found it, so it is ready for the next person to use. Period.

When I was a young teenager, the leader of our Boy Scout troop, Paul "Big Iron" Thompson, enforced a similar ethic at each campsite we visited. Part of our weekend agenda on every trip was listed as "campsite improvement." The motto behind this action was to always "leave it better than you found it."

This might involve picking up sticks or repairing a picnic bench. As kids, we wondered about this rule. Would it not be enough to leave it as good as you found it? And even that seemed kind of strict; we would not trash the place, but would anyone really care if things were slightly worse than we found it when we left?

Eventually though, you look back and realize that "Big Iron" was teaching us something about inhabiting a world of excellence. Remember the "box-checking" mentality of the Compliant level of preparation from the previous chapter? Leaving it "good enough" is what box-checkers do. Without me knowing it, my Scout leader was ingraining a great mindset into my growing brain.

There are many small actions each and every day that put a choice in front of us. If we constantly dismiss little chances to act with character as "small stuff that doesn't really matter," we are building an unproductive habit of mind.

Rewards are a Byproduct, Not the Main Point

Especially when we are young, there is a tendency to think: "If only I had money, status, and power, my life would be good and settled." By this way of thinking, it is the rewards that create a good life.

As understandable as that thinking is, it is exactly backwards. A good life happens when you inhabit a world of excellence first. When you invest in preparation and then execute on your process, you become a person of accomplishment.

That dedication to excellence will generate rewards over time, but those rewards are a byproduct of that excellence, not the point.

One thing that comes to my mind for me is two of my former players. One is quickly rising through the ranks at Oracle, and is no doubt enjoying the rewards that go along with it. The other loved cooking, and studied to become a culinary teacher.

Would we say that the person at Oracle is more successful and has a better life if she is better compensated than the culinary teacher? I would hope not. Each has their own life that they have built through their own character, and they are both reaping the rewards that come from recognizing that Excellence is Its Own Reward.

The true bottom line is this: If you lead a life of excellence, you will have enough tangible rewards to sustain your life and you will be happier. If you chase rewards for their own sake, you may not even get them, and you are definitely putting your happiness at risk.

When I first got out of college, my mindset was very much a "rewards" one. I wanted to pursue wealth and status, basically. Many of the people I was regularly hanging out with were off to a great start in their careers. I wanted that, too, and was worried I was falling behind. I tried to get into construction management, and I did it because I thought it was a way to make money, not because I thought it was what I really should be doing.

Eventually, I fell back on what my parents had taught me: Whatever I chose to do, I should be good at it, no matter the potential money and status (or lack thereof).

With some encouragement from my high school coach, Farrell Rigby (a story I shared in *The Winning Tools*), I decided those dreams of getting rich in construction could be put aside.

But I did not let go of the dream of wanting to be a smashing success—and the sooner, the better. There was no depth to my thinking. I thought I would start coaching, show my stuff, and then before you knew it, I would be the next Pat Riley (the super-successful coach of the Los Angeles Lakers when I was growing up).

At the time, my mind was not so much on the process of learning how to sustain success, but rather on quick success that would raise me to great acclaim. You could summarize it by saying I was hoping for sustained success without having to earn it by learning and implementing the right process, habits, and mindsets.

Of course, my young self would not have put it exactly like that, but my thoughts about how fast and easy success would come were more like an unrealistic dream of a person who had not yet fully matured. I was ambitious, and the good side of that is that I was willing to work very hard. I would sometimes give up my weekends, getting up at 5:00am to drive for hours to attend an all-day coaching clinic.

Ambition had another side, though. I was also focused primarily on my own glory and success, and I would later learn that great leaders need to be focused on how they can help others.

What I did not have yet was the notion that my habits and processes needed to be grounded in the right principles and mindsets.

Please do not misunderstand me. I am not trying to convince you to be a monk and forgo all financial rewards. I do believe in generating tangible results and enjoying the external fruits of that. And I value competition and I do want you to win (both of my books have some form of "Win" in the title, so obviously!).

What I am driving at is that you have to establish the correct order of priority. First, focus on excellence, and the long-term winning and rewards will happen as a result.

This mindset will also help to remind you that not every action is going to have an exactly equal reward immediately. Any time my team was going through a bad patch—maybe a couple of losses or more in a row—I would remind them that we needed to keep our eyes on excellence, and the wins would come.

The Satisfaction of Inhabiting a World of Excellence

Sometimes the pace, pressure, and plain hard work of college basketball coaching made me think: "I would love to go on vacation and live on the beach forever. I would sit in my chair, reach into the cooler for refreshment, and just smile knowing it would never end."

I remember one time when I was feeling like I would love to have one of those permanent vacations, I heard an interview with Lance Armstrong where he said something along the lines of, "There's only so much beer you can drink." His meaning being: There is only so much relaxation you can stand, and fun has an expiration date. Eventually, relaxation and fun become… well, not relaxing and fun.

At the time, I thought, "What in the heck is he talking about? That is idiotic."

However, in time, I began to understand it. Whatever poor choices Lance Armstrong may have made in other areas, I think he got this exactly right.

If I am on vacation, it is enjoyable to a point. If it goes on too long, though, I begin to miss the daily habits that drive excellence.

This is different from being a workaholic. A person who is addicted to work rarely takes vacations, and can be downright compulsive about needing to work to keep other things at bay.

What I am talking about is beginning to miss fully inhabiting a world of excellence. Once you have created the habit of mind to always drive toward excellence, it becomes your source of happiness and satisfaction.

You eventually get the insight: I am now a changed person and I inhabit a different world now. My satisfaction and happiness come from understanding that Excellence is Its Own Reward.

I do want to acknowledge that no one is perfect at this (obviously including myself). If you do something that falls below the standards of excellence in your behavior toward yourself or others, recognize it, learn from it, and then move on. Keep striving to do it more than not, and you will slowly transform. Inhabiting a world of excellence will become an established part of your character.

PREPARATION AND EXCELLENCE

Driving toward excellence is like a muscle you are building in your mind. The more you work it out, the stronger that muscle becomes.

You are going to need that muscle to become a master of preparation. Without it, we have a natural human tendency to want to give ourselves a way to escape the hard work of preparation.

We have that escape if we want it, because great preparation does not guarantee a win in any one particular situation. That makes it easier to justify in our own minds giving less than our best effort in preparation. After all, working super-hard at preparation might not create the result we want. So, maybe let's hedge our bets and not give it our all.

I am not even saying that we always consciously think this way, but it is a subtle thing that does keep many people from committing to excellence.

However, everything changes if you build your Excellence is Its Own Reward muscle, because then all the preparation you do is not about winning in any given situation. It is about preparing at your maximum capacity, because excellence is just what you do. It is who you are.

Note to the Reader: *At the end of each chapter, you will find a brief story that illustrates the key point of the chapter in a specific business context. While these stories are not literally true, I believe most readers will be able to see themselves in them and be better able to appreciate and apply important takeaways.*

"WE REALLY NEED THIS OUTCOME!"

Mark has a problem. He is the CEO of InnovateTech, a software development firm focused on cybersecurity solutions. The business is doing "okay," but Mark is dissatisfied and can sense he is not connecting with his team in a way that drives growth.

InnovateTech entered the market amidst fierce competition and rapidly evolving technological advancements. Mark has been focused on getting his team to understand the tangible outcomes needed to survive and thrive in their niche. His typical drumbeat is a constant emphasis on meeting the goals for profits, market share, and growth metrics.

Mark realizes that knowing these key benchmarks and measuring the company against them is crucial for understanding what is (and is not) working, but he also senses that some key ingredient in his leadership is missing. The message he is constantly sending his team is, "We *really* need this outcome!" That message creates some pressure to get things done, but it does not seem to be unlocking the team's full potential.

Mark begins to question his own mindset and the mindset he is instilling in his team. He asks himself:

- Is my hyper-emphasis on outcomes stealing focus from practical ways to create day-to-day excellence?
- Does my team first think about processes and habits that will create better products and services, or are they mostly just aware of the pressure to drive an outcome?
- If market conditions beyond our control create a temporary profit windfall, is that success? Similarly, if growth is stymied one quarter because of an unexpected downturn in external conditions, should that be considered failure?

After some deep consideration, Mark decides to try something. He will continue to share goals and metrics and progress with the team, but not with the same steady drumbeat.

Instead, he is going to change the focus to creating excellence. Mark makes a conscious and committed decision to the following points:

- He will now emphasize to his team that ALL actions matter—both big and small. Things like: How the team treats each other, customers, and outside vendors on a daily basis; and how accountable everyone is for meeting deadlines and being honest about problems. It will be these little details of character that begin to create a daily atmosphere of excellence.

- Each meeting will now begin not with a recap of outcomes and goals, but with one question: How can we create more excellence in our company? This question will definitely be applied to creating better software and generating first-class service for customers—but it will go deeper, too, and focus on excellence in mindsets, habits, and processes. Talking about excellence and how to drive it will simply become a normal part of life at InnovateTech.
- Mark also commits himself to emailing each member of his leadership team on Monday morning with two questions: What will you do to inhabit a world of excellence this week? What will you ask your departmental team to do this week to drive excellence?

As Mark implements these commitments, he starts noticing a change in his team. Of course, it takes some time, but the shift in mindset creates rewards. On a practical level, the outcomes Mark always wanted now begin to happen more naturally as a byproduct of the focus on excellence. In fact, many of the goals are now exceeded on a regular basis.

Less tangibly but just as importantly, InnovateTech becomes a better place to work. The team is less stressed and more creative in generating new ideas and solving problems. People also make the shift to seeing each other as teammates focused on one thing: Creating and inhabiting a world of excellence together.

MINDSET #2:
BELIEF IN SUSTAINED SUCCESS

NHABITING A WORLD OF EXCELLENCE IS A GREAT FOUN-
dation. You can build on that by adding a rock solid belief in
your own ability to sustain success.

To get a firmer grasp on how to do this, it can be helpful
to imagine a mindset as a filter you put on your thought processes. A healthy mental filter is one that screens out unproductive thoughts and keeps you grounded in reality.

To flesh this out more, think of the filter you have in your
own brain around how you process defeat.

For example, everyone knows that in the world of sports, upsets happen every day: Big ones and small ones; in championship games and in the ordinary regular season games; and everything in between.

I recall in 2012 when we lost a game at Alabama. That year, Kentucky finished first in the SEC with a record of 13-3, and Alabama finished last at 3-13. Worst beat first. As that old sports saying has it, "On any given night..."

This small, simple example points to something much larger about how we define success. I do not remember precisely how I reacted, but I am sure I was not particularly happy about us losing (and obviously it is still in my memory!).

However, we only lost three conference games all year in the SEC.

That was sustained success for the season. It came out of a culture built on the Winning Tools and a relentless commitment to preparation. I mean no disrespect to Alabama at all, but in that particular season, I would rather have been us, no matter the outcome of one game.

In essence, whatever rare upset we suffered, our belief in our ability to maintain sustained success did not waver. The filters we had on our thought processes around defeat were healthy.

Now pause and be honest for a moment. Think of a recent "loss" or setback you had in your work life. It could be big or small.

Was there something you could have reasonably done to avoid it, or some way you could have generated a different outcome?

How did you handle it emotionally and how did you think about it? Did you beat yourself up beyond all recognition? Did you let it roll a little too quickly off your back and not take any lesson from it?

One of the key reasons why the right mindsets are so important is that they keep you from wasting energy on unproductive activities. If your tendency is to overemphasize and overreact to setbacks, you are wasting energy focused on the outcome instead of thinking, "What processes can we improve to become better prepared for the next situation?"

Whether it takes the form of an internal pity party or relentless inward criticism, you are robbing yourself of time and energy you could be spending getting ready to win the next time.

Instead of drowning in unhelpful negativity, I recommend *honestly* analyzing a defeat for what you can learn from it. Learning to do this equips you with a valuable tool for improving your next performance. The lesson learned will direct your vision to a forward path. You will move on to your next challenge with the confidence gained from a lesson learned, not with pointless hand wringing that makes you feel less confident.

Think of it this way: Perspective is your attitude toward an outcome, good or bad. An honestly evaluated defeat leads to proper perspective.

If you suffer from a bad filter about how you process defeats, it is possible to change it. You absolutely can develop a belief in sustained success—and the stronger you make that belief, the further you will go.

DEVELOPING YOUR BELIEF IN SUSTAINED SUCCESS

Let me give you a three-step process for creating a habit of mind that will reinforce the belief that "I am a person of sustained success."

Step 1: Define Success

You have to think hard about how you define success. You need to do this both in the overall sense of who you want to be as a person, as well as for specific situations.

As a person, you need to think about what really matters to you, and make sure your idea of success is something that will truly make you happy. I have found that there is tremendous intrinsic value and satisfaction when I deploy my gifts in a manner that adds value to the world.

The best place to start is honestly recognizing the unique set of gifts you have as a person. When you recognize and acknowledge your gifts, you can then take the next step and identify where you can best use your gifts to contribute your very best to the world.

Ask yourself: What value can you bring, and does it fill you with satisfaction to deliver that value to others? Get clear on what success means to you.

This does not just apply for big definitions of success. When you are facing specific situations and goals, you can apply a similar process. If you are running a major team project, would you say that every team member has a clearly defined vision of what success looks like when the project is completed?

If not, how can you expect your team to achieve success that is not clearly defined?

Always know where your North Star is, and be able to communicate it. Hazy visions and unclear expectations will crush any belief in sustained success.

Step 2: Test Your Definition of Success Against Reality

Dwelling too much on negative outcomes is one enemy, but another is having an unattainable vision of success. Pie-in-the-sky hopes are not "being positive," they are just being unrealistic.

This can be a particular problem for leaders, because people are better at detecting insincerity than you would think. If you don't believe the goal you are setting can be achieved, your people will quickly sniff that out.

Had I started every pre-season speech with, "This year, we are going to win the national championship," I would lose credibility.

If a small e-commerce site CEO says, "In two years, we are going to exceed Amazon in sales," no one will want to climb aboard.

But if that same CEO said, "In this small product niche that we are going to put all our efforts into, we are going to be in the top 5 in our market in sales in two years," that is likely to be much more credible.

For any vision of success, large or small, ask yourself a simple question: Do I really believe that this is an attainable goal?

If not, go back to Step 1 and define success in a way that is challenging but realistic.

Step 3: Decide To Believe in Yourself

At first blush, this step might sound a little more like wishful thinking than a serious step toward success. Decide to believe in yourself and then sustained success will just happen?

Of course, this step is not enough all by itself—but I also think that many people underestimate the role of committing to a decision to believe in yourself.

We all know that challenges are inevitable, and they have a chance to derail us. When adversity strikes, there are two main paths we can take.

Path #1 is to start letting doubts and anxieties overwhelm us, or at least waste our energy to the point that it impacts our preparation and performance. Most people do not actively choose this path, but instead do some version of just letting it happen to them. However, that is still a choice. To make no decision is to choose this path by default.

Path #2 is to choose to believe in yourself and your ability to create sustained success. What exactly does that mean, though?

One thing I like to do when thinking through fundamental principles is go to the dictionary and look up the key word of the principle.

According to Webster's Dictionary, *belief* is a noun which means "acceptance that something is true."

Using this definition, we can say that belief in sustained success is accepting that you have the necessary skills, talent, and developmental abilities to enjoy consistent and long-term accomplishments. To accept something is to say, "Yes, I am taking responsibility for this belief and affirming that it is true."

Make this decision now and affirm it consistently: The best version of yourself is enough to attain long-term success.

You might be a new leader unsure of that, but remember that at least one person thought enough of you to hire or promote you to that position. If you are a seasoned leader facing a new kind of complexity, you have solved other issues and found your way through. You will do it again.

WHAT IS THE CONVERSATION IN YOUR HEAD?

What blocks people from making the decision to believe in their ability to generate sustained success?

Bad mindset habits. If you have them, it is time to start breaking them.

The way you do that is to pay close attention to the conversation going on in your head. Over the next week, make a conscious effort to look at how you process challenges that arise at work.

- How much time do you spend complaining, either out loud or in your head?
- How much time do you spend worrying about circumstances that you cannot control?
- Do you frequently think chaotically and work through problems piecemeal, as if you are fighting one brush fire after another?

If these are your habits of mind, you are convincing yourself that circumstances outside of your control are in charge of your life instead of you.

It is true that circumstances change, and they sometimes do impact us in ways that are beyond our control.

Just because you can make a good and justified complaint does not make it a good use of your time! In fact, it is definitely always a waste of time to spend time nursing and rationalizing complaints. You have problems to solve and key moments to prepare for instead.

The way out is to stop the negative thoughts outlined above. You interrupt those old patterns and retrain your brain in new habits.

- When you start complaining, stop and make a list of practical changes you could make to be better prepared to counteract whatever you are complaining about.
- When you catch yourself worrying about circumstances beyond your control, interrupt yourself and ask: What is one action I could take right now to be better prepared for my next work challenge? And then take that action.
- If you find yourself always trying to solve problems like you are fighting fires, ask yourself: What principles could I be using to categorize these problems and solve them permanently? (Hint: If you are stuck, the Winning Tools are a good and proven set of principles!)

Another way to think about this is in terms of the content you feed your mind.

When resetting your mindsets, what you let run around free inside your brain does matter. Train yourself to follow your thoughts and discern the content that you are feeding your brain. If your content is all about complaints and the impact of external forces, that is like feeding your brain a steady diet of junk food. You can choose different content. It just takes effort and time.

There is one last mindset left to set the foundation. You need to teach your brain to have a consistent, reliable framework for mastering the art of preparation.

"I NEED TO TAME THE CONVERSATION IN MY HEAD"

Newly minted marketing director Alyssa is struggling. She has been with Clarkston Manufacturing for seven years, but it was just three months ago that she was promoted to leading a team. At 34, she is proud to have earned the title at a relatively young age, but Alyssa also feels a little uneasy about it. Is she seasoned enough to succeed in this job?

The CEO of Clarkston, Jane, promoted her over a handful of others who had more tenure. Jane told Alyssa it was a combination of her hard work and her consistently creative ideas that had elevated her above other candidates.

It was true. Her journey so far had been marked by determination and ambition. Soon after she was hired, Alyssa quickly proved herself with innovative campaign ideas and a knack for understanding market trends. She climbed the ladder over the years, taking on more responsibilities and challenges. Each step had its own set of hurdles, but this promotion felt different. It carried the weight of expectations she wasn't sure she could meet.

Now she had her first big test, which was to present a new marketing strategy for the upcoming fiscal year to the CEO and the rest of the executive team. Instead of putting her full focus, energy, and creativity on the strategy and her presentation, Alyssa found herself procrastinating.

If she was honest, it felt like a large portion of her day was spent having a conversation in her own head, mostly about trying to avoid vaguely defined negative outcomes and questioning her ability to run a team.

Finally, she told herself, "Enough! This is not productive. I need to look at what is really going on inside my head and why I am procrastinating." She closed her office door, got out a legal pad and pen, and started thinking about what the real problems were.

After running through some ideas, she wrote down her first conclusion: "I need to tame the conversation in my head." Alyssa decided to stop asking the question, "What happens if I cannot get this done?"

Instead, she would ask action-oriented questions like, "What is one thing I can do right now to advance this strategy?" or, "Who on the team can I assign a specific, productive action to carry out?"

In this way, Alyssa immediately began noticing a shift away from worry and procrastination to practical action, which spiked her confidence.

She also came to a second conclusion: Someone (in this case, the CEO) had believed she could do this job. Why not focus on that external, objective evaluation instead of vague concerns that only existed inside her own head?

Perhaps she would not hit a home run on her first crack at a marketing strategy. Alyssa made the firm decision to aim for long-term career success and not put the weight of the world on one presentation, no matter how important.

As it happened, when it came time to present her marketing strategy, she did get a few bruises. A few of the executives pointed out potential flaws. Alyssa fielded a few tough questions she could have been better prepared to answer.

The executive team asked her to go back and make some significant changes to address their concerns, but they also indicated that the core of the plan was solid.

Alyssa left the presentation feeling like she had just taken a leap forward in her understanding of leadership and success. She had not been perfect or earned a total win on her first big leadership task.

But the understanding she'd received was even better: A confidence that she could handle setbacks, learn from them, and build a career based on choosing to believe she could generate sustained success.

△

MINDSET #3:
COMMITMENT TO
CONSTANT PREPARATION

ULTIPLE CHOICE OR ESSAY?

I remember certain days in high school when I would enter a classroom and that would be the exact question I was anxiously wondering in my head. Was the test that day going to be multiple choice or was it going to be an essay?

I was not prepared for either, but I pinned my faint hopes on a multiple choice test. That at least would allow me to guess, or maybe see some answers that would prompt me to remember something from a previous class.

An essay test, though? That would be the death of all hope. I would not be able to bluff my way through that. My lack of preparation meant nothing I could do on test day would make any difference.

It could have all been different, of course. There was every chance to be prepared. The tests were not a surprise—the teacher announced them in advance. So, I knew the goal (to do well on tests), and I knew exactly when I would need to be ready.

I could have started with the result I wanted (to get a good grade) and then worked backward from that goal to figure out ways to be prepared. Off the top of my head, here are a few options I could have implemented:

- I knew which chapters in our textbook would be on a test. I could have formed a study plan, reviewing a chapter a night or something similar.
- I could have gone personally to the teacher a week before and asked him for advice on how to prepare.
- I could have asked some of the most successful students in the class to form a study group and learned from them the practical study habits of excellent students.

I am sure I could have come up with several more had I applied myself to this kind of thinking. At that age, however, when it came to academics, my mindset did not solve problems in that way.

I did not yet have a habit of mind that oriented me toward a practical preparation plan. What I needed was a mindset that automatically turned me toward creating a method of preparation.

That is what this chapter is all about: Training your brain to follow a method for taking on all problems, projects, and goals like a master of preparation.

To lay the foundation for this, the first thing to do is clear out any false ideas that may block you. Here are three common false beliefs about success and preparation that often trip people up:

- **False Belief:** Others have some special talent that allows them to outperform you.
- **False Belief:** There is *one* answer, a master key to success, and you just have to figure that out and then you will be golden.
- **False Belief:** You need the pressure of a deadline to perform your best.

What all these false beliefs have in common is that they have a vague, undefined quality to them. We tell ourselves that somebody "has more talent than me." Okay, some people may be more talented, but we never really nail that down by asking additional questions, such as, "What is that person doing that I am not, and might that have something to do with their success?" or, "What specific steps can I take to develop my talents?" or, "Is it really all talent, or am I just being outworked by that person?"

Instead of diving deeper, we prefer to leave it as a vague feeling that the other person is just luckier than us in the talent department.

Another problem is telling ourselves there is *one* answer out there somewhere in the universe that we need to find—some secret knowledge that separates the truly great from the rest of the mere mortals. Once we have it, then we will always know what to do, and that will finally be the time to start working hard on preparation.

Of course, what that one answer might look like is extremely hazy, and the path to finding it is even fuzzier. Here again, we often fail to hold our own feet to the fire. Instead of looking for one magical answer, we should be asking what practical steps we can take to observe great leaders and emulate their actions.

The other common false belief is that we need the pressure of a deadline to create good work.

It is true that knowing a deadline is essential for creating a preparation plan—but does that mean that waiting until the last minute spurs maximum creativity? Or, is it more likely that rushing to meet a deadline will lead to a check-the-box mentality because you "just need to get this done?"

Even if you have convinced yourself you need a deadline to create good work, why does it have to be one big, looming deadline? What would be wrong with a series of planned out mini-deadlines that allowed you to do calm, focused work instead of frantic preparation crammed into too small a place? Again, that question is never asked or answered.

I think the reason we live with these half-formed, unclear thoughts about preparation is because we can then tell ourselves it is not completely our fault when we show up unprepared. In a way, we are subconsciously protecting ourselves from the pain of failure. By this way of thinking, we are excused from using the Honesty tool to full effect, since we are never clear on specifics.

Of course, when we are caught out unprepared, we may start beating ourselves up mercilessly for our procrastination—but by then it is too late, and not helpful to our mental state. When we needed to be clear and accountable was earlier.

In short: We need to get crystal clear on our thinking and planning when it can still impact whether we would be powerfully positioned to win.

WHEN I LEARNED THERE WAS NO SECRET

When I started out at the high school coaching level, I figured there was some secret coaching knowledge, and all I had to do was crack the code on that. From there, it would be nothing but acclaim, championships, and easy street success.

I should say that this search for the one secret code of coaching greatness did serve me well in one way. It may have been misguided in its aim, but it did make me work hard looking to connect with people and resources that could make me better. Over time, I learned a lot from this seeking.

This search for the secret went on through four years of coaching at the high school level, and I still could not find the one thing that would provide a seismic shift and hand me the keys to non-stop success.

Then, I was fortunate enough to get hired as a graduate assistant coach for the best coach on the planet at the time, Pat Summit. As I observed her and her practices, it finally dawned on me: I was not going to find one huge answer.

Because there is not one.

I have been asked a thousand times some version of "What did you learn from Pat Summit?" or "How was she so successful?" Behind that question is the assumption that there is some secret or ingredient that amazingly successful people have access to, but the rest of us mere mortals do not.

I do not blame people for that assumption. As I said, I was looking for the same thing. To some degree, it can allow us to let ourselves off the hook for our inaction today. We tell ourselves we will take action at some future point when the secret code has shown us the shining path.

That is not how Pat Summit thought or acted. She was not waiting around for the answer to descend on her. At the most basic level, what she did was simple: Every day, she showed up with a consistent mindset on how the University of Tennessee approached the game of basketball. The key words in that previous sentence are: *Every day.*

By the habits she created around practice and her program, she instilled that same "every day" ethic in her assistants and players.

When you are around greatness, what you see is *the consistency.* I suppose you could call that a secret, but I do not think of it as some mysterious code. It was not about one action or one thought. She just kept herself and her team laser-focused on what mattered most for creating a winning basketball team. When practice started, she was fully present.

There is not some secret otherworldly knowledge that has been cracked by the great coaches. It is the everyday habits. It is believing in being the best prepared person on the court, at the office, or on a sales call. Wherever you ply your craft, if you do that, it is going to lead to amazing success.

"IF I WORK HARDER THAN I DID YESTERDAY, THEN GOOD THINGS WILL HAPPEN"

I had the great opportunity to interview my friend Ben Graham, founder and CEO of Graham Family Capital, about some of the ingredients to his remarkable success.

In the fall of 2023, Ben sold his company after serving as CEO and President for Bell, Incorporated, a packaging and containers business located in South Dakota. In his time as CEO, Ben more than 10x'ed Bell's revenue, taking it from $18 million in sales to $200 million+.

What role has hard work and preparation played in your success?

"My dad Mark Graham had a motto that soaked into my own brain from a young age: 'If I work harder than I did yesterday, good things will happen.' He often said he was not the smartest guy, but he would be the hardest working.

"A big part of that hard work always involved planning and preparation. In 1976, my dad was selling insurance and making a good living, but he wanted something where he could control his own destiny and go further. At the time, he was scouting a business to buy, and was meeting with a weekly group of successful people to bounce ideas off of them.

"Eventually, he narrowed it down to two: A horseradish farm (of all things!) or a small packaging business with outdated equipment. He thought through the implications. People would likely always buy horseradish, and it seemed steady, but is there any way to massively grow a horseradish business?

"My dad freely admitted he did not have in-depth knowledge of the packaging business, but he did see there could be pathways to exponentially grow in that industry. It was a combination of carefully considering the potential implications of each, but also being willing to make a decision and count on hard work to help him figure it out."

I know you went to work at your dad's company and eventually you won a contract with McDonald's. How did that happen?

"I was involved in the business growing up, and then began a full-time position in 1997 after getting a degree from the University of Montana. I began in sales, and it was a natural fit for me. I loved all of it, the craft of selling, building relationships, creating value—all of it.

"At some point, I was ready for a change from living in South Dakota and I moved to Chicago. McDonald's had headquarters there, and I told my dad that I was going to get a contract from them to source some of their packaging through us.

"He was skeptical to say the least, but I was relentless. I was young and did not have a ton of money back then, and so I was living scrappy. My house was robbed twice in the first six months I lived there. Whatever the setbacks, I joined a local health club and started playing basketball with a bunch of professionals, lawyers, MBAs, folks like that, and trying to make friends and network in those ways.

"I was extremely persistent about attempting to get in front of McDonald's. I just kept trying to reach out and find doorways, contacts, anything I could do. It was a little bit of the classic sales advice, 'I won't take no for an answer.'

"We finally got our foot in the door, and they gave us a shot. It all started with a relatively small contract for just over a million dollars to produce their french fry containers for four of their Midwest distribution centers.

"Finding and landing a client like McDonald's was part of a planned strategy. With a company like ours, you could service 500 businesses and try to keep them all happy. Or you could find some selective Fortune 500 companies and get in with them and then keep growing with them. That seemed a much smarter way to prepare and plan for the future.

"Of course, getting a first contract is only a first step. If you want to stay on with a big company, you have to earn it. You have to out-service any competition and be just as competitive or better on cost structure. All that takes planning and execution.

"We were able to grow right along with McDonald's as we built that trust and service with them."

How did the transition to CEO happen for you? What role did preparation play?

"As I said, I loved sales, but I also knew that someday I would want to move into the role of CEO, and I knew that only understanding one slice of the business was not good enough.

"I realized I would need to be proactive about educating myself on every important facet of business. I also thought that Bell, Inc. had reached a level of revenue where it could get complacent. If you want to grow an already mature business and keep busting through ceilings, it requires more knowledge than I had from just sales.

"I was admitted to an amazing weekend MBA program at Northwestern. This school was above my academic record, but I got in through a combination of luck, connections, perfect timing, and my business experience. It meant giving up whole weekends for two years, but it was amazing preparation for my role.

"I continued to drive myself to understand different areas of the business so when the day came, I would be ready. It happened in 2009, and I was still young to be a CEO at age 30. But all that tenacious preparation up to that point had set me up well."

What are you doing now that you've sold Bell, Inc.?

"I am on a sabbatical for about a year to enjoy focusing on my family and maximizing my health. Currently, I have an excellent leader guiding Graham Family Capital. When it turns to the new year, I am going to focus on what is next for the business. I am going to do it the way I always have done it. I am going to get clear on three kinds of planning: Short-term, medium-term, and long-term. This kind of detailed planning and preparation are indispensable for success."

One final note on this interview: Near the end, I was happily surprised to hear the tagline Ben had chosen for Graham Family Capital. It was the exact phrase I have been using so often in this book. The tagline? Sustained Success.

OVERVALUING GREATNESS

There is a tendency to overvalue a mythical quality of "greatness" in our minds. We see amazing success from far away. We read about it online or in magazines, or watch great championships or fantastic business success play out on our screens or in the books we read.

We can simply say, "That person is just one of those types of people who has 'it,'" or, "They had the right background or the right set of skills." There is even a partial truth to that. Some people do have more talent, and some people did have some advantages or breaks.

However, I also think there is a danger we can fall into if we idolize greatness. We can build that other person up so much in our minds that we think of them as some kind of superhuman we can just look at in awe, without getting anything of practical value out of it. These idols become just a source of vague inspiration, and nothing more.

Instead, what if we said, "I may or may not become [super-successful person you admire], but I wonder what specific actions and mindsets I could learn from them?"

You do not have to be one of the greatest ever in your chosen field to be an amazing leader. You can create mindsets that allow you to reach your full potential, whatever that is. This also creates the possibility that you might just rise to become one of the greats yourself.

Never assume that some people have "it" and you just do not. Do not let yourself overvalue greatness to that degree.

To summarize the two key points in this chapter so far:

- **There is no code to crack.** It is about training yourself in good habits, focus, and hard work.

- **Get rid of beliefs about vague formulas for success.**
  Start thinking in terms of specific, detailed preparation
  plans, not some hazy ideas about greatness.

TRANSLATING THESE IDEAS INTO A MINDSET OF CONSTANT PREPARATION

Every task, situation, or project is different and unique, right?
Of course it is—and your preparation plans for each specific
circumstance will need to be unique, too.

However, there is also something common to every kind
of task, situation, or project. To be more precise, I should say
there is something that *should* be in common between them all.

What should be consistent is the framework of how you
approach preparation.

This is an absolutely crucial habit of mind to get into
your head if you want to become a person of great preparation. When you have something to accomplish, there may be
a bunch of scattered factors flying at you. As we said before,
the further you climb up the ladder of leadership, the more
complex things will get.

However, if you have a set framework in your mind to
approach whatever is in front of you, you will be the center of
calm preparation for whatever you and your team face.

Let's call it the **Framework of Constant Preparation.**
Those who learn it and make it their everyday approach to

attacking projects, tasks, and situations will always be in a powerful position to win.

At a high level, it looks like this:

Clarity of Goal

What is my goal? What specific markers will tell me I have been successful on this task or project?

To get to that goal, what subgoals have to be met along the way? This concept of **subgoals** is vital for creating step by step success, a way to reverse engineer the results you want.

We will cover this in more depth in the next chapter—but for now, let me illustrate with a very simple example.

Let's say you need 20 closed deals a month to meet your revenue goals. You know that your sales close rate when you can meet with a prospective customer is 50%. That gives you your first subgoal: You need to have 40 quality leads a month to close 20 sales. Now take it another step back. For simplicity, let's say you get all of your leads through cold calling, and your team averages one quality lead for every 50 calls. Putting this together, that means 2,000 cold calls a month will generate 40 quality leads. Now you have another subgoal. Each subgoal is a link in the chain that gets you to your big goals.

Once you are clear on goals and subgoals, it is time to think in terms of strategy.

Create a Strategy

Here are some good questions for formulating a strategy:

- Have I achieved this goal before, and if so, how?
- How have others achieved this same goal, and how did they do it?
- What is essential to this, and what is not?
- What are the strengths of my team, and does my strategy play to those strengths?

Write Out a Plan

Use your strategy to create a detailed, written plan that guides you and your team through the preparation that gets you ready to win. Writing it out is important; it makes it more real.

Your written plan will be in scale to the situation or project. For big, audacious goals, this will be an extensive plan that takes time and covers all the essentials in a complete way.

For your personal daily plan focused on the specific day ahead of you, setting aside a few minutes to create key bullet points can often be enough.

DEEPLY EMBED THIS FRAMEWORK IN HOW YOU APPROACH EVERYTHING

Ingrain these steps for everything you need to accomplish or solve. If your brain gets into this essential pattern, you will be breaking complexity down into a highly productive framework that will not fail you.

Let's repeat it one more time to help start the process of making it a bedrock habit of your mind:

The Framework of Constant Preparation

1. Get clarity on your goals and subgoals.
2. Figure out what your strategy will be for reaching each goal.
3. Write out a plan using your chosen strategy to guide the details.

This three-step rhythm gets you ready to win... and then ready to win again and again.

THE MOUNTAIN

Here is a simple metaphor that many people have found helpful in understanding the power of this mindset.

Every time you have an audacious goal, think of being at the base of a mountain. Your goal is at the top of that mountain. You create your plan for getting to the top of the mountain, which will be a series of climbs and milestones along the way.

Once you have a plan, forget about the top of the mountain. Put all your efforts into executing each step up that mountain.

Focus on the first milestone. Then the next one. Then the one after that.

Each milestone is another step forward in your preparation. If you created a good plan, then each milestone is getting you closer until you reach the top of the mountain.

On the flip side, if your "plan" is only to focus on the top of the mountain, frustration can begin to set in. It is easy to get discouraged or intimidated looking up all the way to the top of the mountain.

Here are two simple but helpful questions to ask if you are getting anxious or procrastinating instead of preparing:

- Have I created a clear plan with milestones for reaching the top of this mountain?
- If yes, do I know what the next milestone up the mountain is? Am I focused on that milestone? Is my team aware and focused on that milestone?

Use this simple mental visualization of a mountain as a quick reminder and reinforcement of this mindset.

READ THE NEXT THREE CHAPTERS CAREFULLY...

As you progress through the next three chapters, I want you to think back to this chapter and notice something. The upcoming chapters line up precisely with the Framework of Constant Preparation.

Chapter 5 is about getting clarity on your goals and subgoals. That is what you want to get super-clear on. The goal is the top of the mountain, and the subgoals are each milestone along the way.

Next, Chapter 6 is about figuring out the strategies you will use to reach those goals. This is the focus you need to reach each of those milestones. You are not straining to see the top of the mountain; instead, you are focused on the "how" of reaching each specific subgoal.

Finally, Chapter 7 is about taking action on those strategies by creating a detailed plan and executing it. Taking action is when the mindset gets deeply ingrained. You and your team know exactly what you are working on and why, and momentum builds. Then you understand that preparation powerfully positions you to win—and as you win more often, the value is reinforced again. It is a tremendously effective cycle.

The readers who will get the most out of this book are those that see the connection between a mindset of constant preparation and the practical framework lived out every day.

So, let's dive deeper to see how this all comes together.

"IT WAS NEVER ABOUT SOME MYTHICAL QUALITY OF GREATNESS"

Jake should have been thrilled. He had just been hired as the Vice President of Sales at Culinarium, a well-established chain of restaurants known for its innovative fusion cuisine. If you had told him ten years ago that he would get this job, he would have been "out of his mind" excited!

But now that he had it, he was immediately worrying about his next step. Jake had a tendency to be restless. On each rung of the ladder of his career, he immediately started looking at the next rung up. He always knew that long-term, he wanted to be a CEO at a consequential company.

Now that he was getting close to that top rung, it made him wonder whether he could ever get there.

If he was thinking straight, Jake would realize he had a perfect opportunity to find out by observing one of the best. He would be directly reporting to Culinarium's legendary founder and CEO, Micah.

Micah had already built a successful restaurant empire previously to Culinarium, and he had been regularly featured in mainstream business publications like Fortune, Forbes, and Inc.

Jake was ready to take his front row seat and learn from Micah, but with some reservations. There was a part of Jake that figured he would always live in the shadows of the "Micahs" of the world. There were just certain business leaders who had "it," some greatness or charisma that could not be replicated or equaled by mere mortals.

Jake considered himself talented, hardworking, and a good learner. He felt he could be CEO material, but maybe not someone who could rise to be the "best of the best" in the CEO category.

It took a few months in his VP role for Jake to start to change his mind about greatness and how to achieve it. He observed Micah closely at every opportunity, and tried to understand how he thought and communicated.

Micah did have some natural charisma for sure, and he talked with the confidence of someone who had built two huge restaurant chains—but he was also human, and some of the ideas he proposed occasionally sounded less than brilliant to Jake (although there were some great ideas, too).

Micah also clearly and openly relied on his Chief Operating Officer for crucial functions because they did not play to his strengths.

However, the biggest things that caught Jake's attention about Micah were not his weaknesses, and not his charisma. What made Micah stand out were his habits and processes. In fact, he was as disciplined a person in these areas as anyone Jake had ever seen.

During meetings, Micah's ability to listen intently and ask incisive questions was prominent. He did not try to dominate discussions, but encouraged diverse viewpoints and collaborative problem-solving. However, once he had made a decision, he was very methodical and precise in making clear what the goals were and who was responsible for what.

Micah was careful about his schedule, including building in time for exercise and mental breaks during the day. He only checked his email once a day, letting his assistant notify him if anything was truly urgent.

One day, Jake and Micah had a one-on-one meeting that ended early. Jake mustered the courage to ask Micah about his journey to success. His response was unexpectedly candid. Micah recounted early setbacks and challenges, emphasizing how each obstacle had been a catalyst for growth. He attributed his achievements not to innate talent, but to resilience, adaptability, and a relentless pursuit of excellence.

Jake's admiration for Micah evolved into deep respect and inspiration. He no longer viewed his success as unattainable, but as a blueprint for his own development. He started implementing small changes in his daily routines—dedicating more time to market research, actively listening to colleagues, and being disciplined about all areas of his schedule.

Over time, these incremental improvements translated into tangible results for Culinarium, boosting sales figures past all expectations. Most importantly for Jake's career, he now knows he is ready to be a CEO when the right opportunity presents itself. It was never about some mythical quality of greatness or figuring out what "it" was.

It was about processes, habits, and a relentless pursuit of excellence.

CLARITY AND GOALS

THE SUMMER BEFORE MY SENIOR YEAR IN HIGH SCHOOL, I was given the remarkable opportunity to attend a football camp for high school quarterbacks run by Bobby Bowden, the head coach of the Florida State Seminoles, who by then was well on his way to legendary status.

Much later in life, I had another wonderful encounter with Coach Bowden when Kentucky football head coach Mark Stoops hosted Coach Bowden for an event in Lexington. Coach Stoops had previously been a defensive coordinator at Florida State, and that connection brought Coach Bowden for a visit. I had the good fortune of being in the room with Coach Bowden that night.

These were two relatively brief encounters separated by decades, but the charisma and leadership abilities were loud and clear in both cases. I had admired him ever since that high school football camp, so I always sat up and took notice when I saw a talk or interview with Coach Bowden.

I remember one particular story he told about his early coaching days at Florida State. When he first got to campus, the resources for the football team were pretty poor.

Facilities were in ugly shape, including old, crumbling locker rooms. The practice fields were terrible, and the program was not exactly overflowing with shiny, new equipment either. I think the majority of people in a position like that would see this as a reason to complain loudly, and it could be a ready-made excuse for losing, too. How many of us would say, "You expect me to win with this!?"

That is not how Coach Bowden looked at it, though. He said that as long as you had enough equipment to suit up, the only thing you should focus on is how to play good football. He knew that as long as he did that, everything else would come in time.

Sure enough, the winning started. His teams won two national championships before he retired. Perhaps even more amazingly, his Seminole team once went 14 consecutive seasons *finishing* in the top 5 of the Associated Press poll. No other team has ever done that more than seven times. That is sustained success with an exclamation point!

Of course, the resources did grow alongside the success. What Coach Bowden knew was the exact right order to put things. Excellence on the field came first. All that energy you save by eliminating complaints can be poured into what really matters.

There are numerous lessons that could be pulled out of this little example—but for the purposes of this chapter I want to drill down into one particular aspect of it, and that is this: Coach Bowden understood the power of having crystal clarity around the main goal.

He was there to teach his team to win, and the lousy practice fields and ugly locker rooms had pretty much zero to do with the techniques, skills, game plans, and conditioning of his players. He knew what the goal was, and it was not to win the award for best facilities.

COACH BOWDEN'S EXCEPTIONAL PRE-SEASON PREPARATION

I had a chance to chat about Coach Bowden with two time SEC Coach of the Year Mark Richt. Coach Richt was an assistant at Florida State for 10 years, including six as Coach Bowden's offensive coordinator. He went on to become an excellent head coach in his own right at University of Georgia and University of Miami. Georgia won two SEC championships with Coach Richt at the helm.

In talking with Coach Richt, I was struck in particular with his description of how meticulous Coach Bowden was in preparing his entire staff during the pre-season.

Coach Bowden always had a coaches all-day retreat right before the season. It was incredibly detailed and covered every important area for the upcoming season, getting clarity on what was needed on the field and off and who was responsible for what.

Coach Bowden did not stop there. He also brought together every single person who had any role in the football program during the pre-season. Coach Bowden would recognize and name each person in front of everyone else and describe their role.

Some coaches who do this kind of thing would stop after recognizing the "most important" staff, but Coach Bowden made a point of acknowledging that everyone mattered.

However, this was about more than just recognition; it also brought a level of clarity and accountability. By naming everyone and outlining their roles and responsibilities, it eliminated confusion. Additionally, it created some positive pressure of accountability on each and every individual. Would you want to let Coach Bowden and everyone else in that championship program down?

A good question to ask yourself as a leader is how you could implement something similar on your team.

> How often do you recognize each person on your team?
> How clear are you with everyone about the clarity of
> their roles? Does everyone know who is accountable
> for what?

THE LOSING TOOLS

In my career, I had a lightning bolt moment that gave me an insight which helped give birth to the Winning Tools.

It happened when I was an assistant at the University of Florida, and we had just finished a bruising 2002–03 season. At the start of the year, we had somewhat high expectations, but finished at 9–19 overall. Head Coach Carolyn Peck, who already had a national championship on her resume, gathered the staff to go through a "no stone unturned" excavation of the season to pull out the lessons we could.

At one point in the conversation, one of the other assistants said, "If we could eliminate complaints, excuses, and laziness, we would really have something."

For whatever reason, those words hit me like an "*Aha!*" moment. I cannot remember who said them, but the phrase itself burned into my memory bank.

In some ways, it seems odd that it struck such a chord at the time. That Florida team did not stand out as a team that was particularly bad about complaints, excuses, or laziness. Of course, we were not happy about our record, but we lost a lot of tough games that year, and the effort was there.

I think the reason it stuck with me was because it captured something universal. Any team—whether in sports or in business—can be held back from achieving sustained success by complaints, excuses, and laziness. For that matter, it holds us back as individuals, too. It is human nature to have tendencies in this direction, and any team or individual that can eliminate them has a huge advantage in being ready to win.

I filed this bit of wisdom away in my memory bank, and three years later, I became the head coach at Morehead State. I needed to come up with a blueprint that would guide us—and as I shared in the first book, this was where I formulated the Winning Tools. Now I want to add to that story by sharing the connection of the Losing Tools to the Winning Tools.

As I thought about the phrase, "complaints, excuses, and laziness," I began thinking of those as the Losing Tools. Since I wanted to win, I asked myself what the opposite qualities were. I refined their connection over the years, and this is how I pair them up:

- Honesty is the opposite of Excuses
- Hard Work is the opposite of Laziness
- Discipline is the opposite of Complaints

When you are practicing radical honesty, you are on a search for the real truth of whatever issue you are solving or goal you are after. When you make excuses, you are not in search of the truth; you are in search of what serves your own self.

It is obvious how laziness is the opposite of hard work.

Complaints are the opposite of discipline because when you use discipline, you are forcing yourself to stay on task to solve a real problem in the real world. On the other hand, when you complain, all your energy is spent doing nothing but venting into the air.

The simplicity of the Winning Tools versus the Losing Tools is an incredibly effective teaching tool for integrating these fundamental concepts into your team or organization. I know this because we used it at Kentucky and I saw my players absorb it deeply into their mindsets over time. I have also seen it work extremely well in workshops.

The way we would teach it is this: "We want to win, and honesty, hard work, and discipline will create it. And here is what will guarantee losing: Complaints, excuses, and laziness."

At Kentucky, we even had laminated cards that each player carried emphasizing this contrast. On one side, in beautiful script and printed in Kentucky blue and white, we had the Winning Tools. On the other, in plain letters printed in drab black and white, we had the Losing Tools.

This served as a constant reminder to the players that all this was a *choice*. One cannot live both philosophies at the same time. If you are making excuses, you are not being honest. If you are being lazy, you are not working hard. If you are complaining, you are failing at discipline. Which side of the card do you want to live by?

Essentially, if you catch yourself living in the Losing Tools, that is a flashing red light signaling that your preparation is off track. You are not using your energy to get ready to win. You are wasting it on basically nothing.

People can immediately resonate with this contrast and see that it is doable. "I can do that. I can be a person of honesty, hard work, and discipline. I can also recognize when I am complaining, making excuses, or being lazy. I will do the former and not the latter."

It is incredibly powerful.

Complaint vs. Concern

I do need to share one thing I learned the hard way with the Losing Tools. You want to stop complaints, but you want to be careful not to stamp out constructive feedback and questions. Early on in my head coaching career, I noticed that when you ban complaining, people will sometimes completely shut down and not bring up valid issues.

So, I taught my players the difference between a complaint and a concern. A complaint is just a negative swirl of energy going nowhere. "Why is Coach making us get up at 6:00am to practice? This stinks, there is no reason for it, I'm so tired."

Compare that to a concern. "Coach, what is the reason we are practicing at 6:00am? Can we move the practice to a later time?"

As a leader, you may not change anything in response to a particular concern (although sometimes you will). However, at a minimum, giving people encouragement to ask good questions and express constructive concerns gives you a chance to explain the reason why you are doing it this way.

THE CLARITY CONNECTION

So far in this chapter, I have strongly contrasted the Winning and Losing Tools because they reveal something important about goals and clarity.

If you and your team spend time on complaining, excuses, and laziness, I can tell you for certain that one of two things is going on:

- You are unclear on what your goal is. *Or...*
- You know the goal, but you do not stay focused on what will get you there.

Let's return this to the story that began this chapter. If Coach Bowden spent his energy complaining about the locker room, that would reveal that his goal was not winning games. His goal would have been *looking* like a program that wins games.

But Bobby Bowden was way too clear on the real goal to fall for that phony one. When you know your true goal with clarity, you see that the Losing Tools have no value.

MORE BENEFITS OF GOAL CLARITY

Besides keeping you away from the Losing Tools, clarity about your goals will teach you when to say "no" to distractions, and when to say "yes" to innovations.

Think of a clear goal as a lens that helps you see better what is a useless diversion versus what is a positive change or addition.

The question is: "Does 'X' move me closer to this goal or help me get there faster?" If yes, then "X" is an innovation worth strongly considering. If the answer is "no," then you know it does not have any essential impact on the overall goal, and you can safely cast it aside as a distraction.

The other huge benefit you will get from goal clarity is energy and excitement. So many organizations and teams struggle with individuals pulling in different directions. This is occasionally a problem with a handful of individuals, but more often it has to do with a lack of clarity.

How much energy is wasted because not everyone is clear on exactly what needs to be accomplished? If you walked up to anybody on your team and asked them for the most essential goals of the organization, how many of them could give a very clear answer?

The energy you can unleash within people and teams when you can set and then communicate a goal clearly is astounding.

METHODS AND CRITERIA FOR SETTING CLEAR GOALS

The first thing I like to do when setting a goal—particularly a team goal where I need others to buy in—is think honestly about whether it is grounded in reality.

Is this goal realistic, or is it based on wish fulfillment?

Many young leaders think that you throw a big, bold goal in front of a team and then challenge them to get there.

One way to accomplish this is to give your team short-term, incremental subgoals that are challenging but feel incremental enough to be doable. Do that enough times and with enough success, and you may discover that you really do get the team to accomplish an audacious goal they did not not think possible when they first started.

Seasoned leaders take into account their resources and team's current development, and set believable goals within those constraints. It is important to remember that one of those constraint factors is timeline. Is it not only possible for your team to accomplish the goal, but also reasonable to expect them to do it in the time set?

Next, you want to determine whether the goal can be measured, and what those measurements should be.

Many people get shy here, typically for two reasons. One is that they claim they are not a "numbers" person, and the second is more often unstated: They are shying away from the accountability and conflict that specific measurements can generate. Let's look at each of these in turn.

As for not being a numbers person, I understand. I am not a mathematically minded person by nature either. Fortunately, though, I worked for Carol Ross at University of Florida for two seasons.

She did not try to change my style and make me a super analytics guy. She did, however, teach me the value of looking at trends and statistical pointers that indicated success. I learned that you did not have to love crunching numbers to set key metrics—it is not nearly as complicated as it is sometimes made out to be.

When it comes to numbers and goals, the secret reason why many people are scared of them is because it makes accountability unavoidable, and that will sometimes mean confronting failure with yourself or others.

Putting a number to something takes the subjectivity out of it, so when you analyze success or failure, you and your team will have to take responsibility for what happened. If you struggle with putting measurables next to goals, reflect on whether this is part of the problem.

In summary, here are two tests you can ask for each goal you set:

Goal Test #1: Is This Goal Credible Given the Available Resources?

As I said, you want to be realistic and reasonable. However, do not go too far and put limits on your team that are not really there. I once heard what the late Steve Jobs—the incredible founder, CEO, and visionary of Apple—had to say on the subject of goals. Jobs made the distinction between what is "seemingly" impossible and what is "truly" impossible. He said you must open your mind to difficult challenges, stretch toward a solution, and truly ascertain whether the goal you are trying to accomplish is, in fact, possible.

It is a good question to ask: Are you limiting your goal because it is only "seemingly" impossible at first blush?

Goal Test #2: Does This Goal Have a Specific Measurable or Data Associated With It? If Not, Why Not?

If you are familiar with the SMART goal setting method, you will notice that these tests cover much the same ground. For those not familiar with SMART (or for those who need a review), it stands for:

- Specific
- Measurable
- Attainable
- Realistic
- Timely

Use the goal tests above or S.M.A.R.T. to create good goals. The basics of what makes for a good goal are fairly well-known. The bigger question is: Are you applying it?

IF YOU WANT TO BE AN EXCEPTIONAL LEADER, YOU NEED TO ABSORB THIS NEXT SECTION

I think a lot of advice about goals falls short in one key area. **There is not enough emphasis on the importance of creating specific subgoals that add up to your larger goals.**

To state it clearly: It is crucial to put as much thought into the milestone accomplishments as it is into your overall goal. Sometimes even more.

The key to all this is reverse engineering. What is your big goal? Okay, now walk back step by step to what will lead to that goal. Keep going until you have a vital set of subgoals that put you in a position to win.

For instance, when I was at Kentucky, one of our key goals in any season was hearing our name called on Selection Sunday.

Historically, we knew that 92% of SEC teams that won eight or more conference games were included in the NCAA tournament. So, we knew our goal was to win a minimum of eight conference games.

Okay, now another step back. What were the indicators that a team would be successful in a conference like the SEC? For one, having a rebounding edge. Because my teams were built on speed and quickness, we tended not to be big and bruising. That meant that dominating the defensive boards was unlikely.

But could we use our quickness to elude blockouts and secure more offensive rebounds?

Or could we use our quickness and defensive scheme to have an excellent turnover margin? If a team is turning the ball over, that means they are taking less shots, and that can make up a rebounding deficit.

In this way, we kept going one more link down the chain, looking for statistical pointers to use as measurables for subgoals. While "eight wins" is a good and clear overall goal, it does not tell you specifically what steps it will take to get there. You piece that together with subgoals.

One of the most powerful aspects of subgoals is that it reminds you that great outcomes are based on a chain of actions, each building and accumulating toward an amazing amount of success.

It is no different in business than in basketball. If you have a sales revenue goal, you also need to have a subgoal to have a certain amount of leads, and it has to be specific. You also need a nailed down subgoal for how many of those leads you can realistically close. The last part of the equation is to know the subgoal for the average amount of each sale.

In this way, you can monitor subgoals for leads, close rate, and average sale amount to see whether you are tracking to "win" at the end of the year by meeting your sales revenue goal.

You can do this with any part of your business. Ask questions like:

- How is each department or person expected to contribute to your overall goal?
- What subgoals do they contribute to the overall goal?
- How is that being tracked?

This breakdown into subgoals is absolutely essential if you want to be a leader of great preparation. Without subgoals, you will not have created a chain of preparation steps leading you to the doorstep of your main goals.

Let's end with an exercise that can get you thinking about creating clear subgoals.

- **Step 1:** Think of a particular challenge or goal that you or your team have been very hit or miss on achieving. Write that challenge or goal down at the top of a piece of notebook paper (or type it into a document if you prefer to work digitally).

- **Step 2:** Then, working your way down the paper, write down the steps that would lead to meeting that goal or solving the problem. Try to work backward from the result and not miss any key steps.

- **Step 3:** Now go back to each key step. What number or measurement could you put next to each step?

> **Reader Bonus:** Go to *coachmatthewmitchell.com/resources* and download the *Ready to Win Journal*. It contains the "Subgoal Mapping" page that provides a solid format for these three steps.

While you may not be able to come up with a perfect plan off the top of your head with this exercise, moving in this direction can give you a feel for the power of subgoals.

Now what you need is a strategy to make those subgoals happen.

"THE ORGANIZATION BECAME A PLACE
OF ENERGY AND PURPOSE"

Dr. Julia Thompson heads up a prominent healthcare organization, HealthSphere. As the CEO, Julia is known for her tenacity and innovative spirit. Despite the company's promising growth, she sensed a persistent undercurrent of confusion and lack of direction within her team. Recent quarterly reviews highlighted a recurring theme: Misaligned goals and unclear responsibilities were holding back progress. This vague confusion seemed to penetrate deep within the organization.

One Monday morning, after a particularly frustrating meeting, Julia decided it was time for a change. She realized she could never steer HealthSphere toward its vision if many team members did not have total clarity on their specific objectives and responsibilities.

Julia decided half measures were not enough. She scheduled a three-day retreat for every executive and manager to attend. Day One would be about getting crystal clear on objectives. Day Two would focus on working back from those objectives to create subgoals that would lead to the results everyone wanted. Day Three would be about assigning clear accountability and action steps for each role in the organization, all aligned with the subgoals that needed to be met.

From there, she asked all these executives and managers to schedule a one-on-one meeting with every single direct report and have a meeting to explain HealthSphere's overall goals, followed by that person's role in helping achieve those objectives.

At the end of 30 days, she wanted signed accountability and subgoal plans from every member of the organization.

Once this was fully implemented, the fog of confusion lifted, and that was when it was revealed just how much a lack of clarity had been holding HealthSphere back.

As HealthSphere's processes and habits improved, so did its outcomes. Patient satisfaction scores rose, operational efficiencies increased, and employee turnover decreased. The organization became a place of energy and purpose, where each team member knew what they were responsible for and how their work contributed to the collective success.

Julia's leadership in addressing the confusion of goals and clarity transformed HealthSphere. Her structured approach to goal setting and accountability, combined with breaking objectives down into incremental steps, created a robust framework for sustained growth and improvement.

Seeing these results, Julia made the three-day goal setting retreat and follow-up a permanent part of HealthSphere's annual activities.

To further deepen and make these changes a part of the company culture, Julia made it a point to celebrate small wins, understanding that recognition was crucial in maintaining the momentum created by the new sense of purpose. These celebrations were not grand, but they were meaningful—a shout-out in a meeting, a thank-you note, or a small team lunch. These gestures all reinforced the importance of each individual's role in the larger mission, and continued to transform HealthSphere.

STRATEGY

NOW IS THE PERFECT TIME TO TAKE A BRIEF PAUSE IN the forward flow and reorient ourselves before we forge ahead.

So far, the steps and key actions can be summarized as:

- Recognize that a "check-the-box" mentality is not enough and choose the committed level of preparation.
- Train your brain with the right habits of mind. You have to interrupt bad mindset habits and replace them with three great mindsets: Excellence is Its Own Reward, Belief in Sustained Success, and Commitment to Constant Preparation.

- You need to get clear on goals, and reverse engineer specific subgoals that create a path to winning and sustained success.

You are committed. Your mind is focused. You are crystal clear on your goals and subgoals. This puts you in the perfect position to think through strategy.

Here are a few questions that can get you thinking in the right direction:

- What central ideas can guide our detailed plan of preparation?
- Given these goals and subgoals, what strategy (or multiple strategies) can get us there?

I will give you an example from college basketball recruiting.

The goal here was pretty clear: You wanted to recruit good players who could help you win. Because if you did not win, eventually you would not have your job.

However, within that overall goal, there are a lot of different factors that come into play. Good players come in all shapes and sizes.

- Some are built on mostly talent and not too much grit.
- Others have superior toughness and enough talent to make it work.

- There are some who are both fantastic athletes and superstars in the classroom, too.
- There are some who will go anywhere that best showcases their talent, and do not need to feel a particular loyalty or connection to a school in order to choose it.
- There are others who are looking for that snug fit between the culture of the team and themselves.

I could probably come up with 100 other distinctions depending on how detailed we wanted to get. And every player is a unique individual, so no one category could completely define anyone.

However, I did need some kind of thought process or strategy for pursuing the kind of player that would best fit Kentucky and flourish there as a player and a human being.

What I wanted was a general set of criteria that would prevent me from spending a lot of time recruiting players who were unlikely to sign with Kentucky. With the number of players available, you had to have some way of getting a handle on the process.

For instance, if a player was both an incredibly high-achieving student and excellent player, they were most likely to end up at schools like Stanford, Cal, Duke, Northwestern, or Vanderbilt. This is not to say Kentucky was not a good school academically or that we did not emphasize academics in our program. Thanks to the support and focus of our Athletic

Director Mitch Barnhart, Kentucky athletics drove excellence in this area across the board.

However, the reality was that a student with that profile was much more likely to go to one of those schools. Spending time finding and recruiting these players was generally not a good use of my limited time.

With experience, I came to see that the players who would come to Kentucky were those who were attracted to the genuine enthusiasm and passion I felt for the program and the people in it.

This helped me eliminate the focus on the position a potential recruit played. Instead, I was looking for a certain passion and an alignment of values. I asked myself, "Is this a person of good character who loves our values?"

I also liked to look for solid players I felt were being undervalued in the recruiting rankings. Some coaches like to focus on particular geographic areas, but I would recruit from anywhere there was a player that would be a good fit and was passionate about coming to the University of Kentucky.

Essentially, the strategy was to focus on players who fit our culture and had the mental makeup to play our relentless style of basketball. Of course, they had to be exceptionally talented and skilled basketball players to play in the SEC—but past that, I focused on passion and enthusiasm.

I also had a strategy that kept me focused on the details of *how* I recruited, not just *who* I recruited. My belief was that my strength in recruiting was making a personal connection with a player and their parents.

So, whenever I thought about any detailed preparation in recruiting, I would think, "Will this particular task help me build a personal connection, or is it more like busy work?" If it did not relate to helping make a personal connection, it was something to de-prioritize or eliminate altogether.

I would also use this strategy to decide how deep to dig into the details. For instance, I always felt like the look of our recruiting presentations was worth sweating over. Why? Because when you are trying to make a connection with someone, the quality and feel of what you present represents you in some way. Having an intentional strategy to "create a personal connection" allowed me to decide, "Yes, this matters."

I should quickly add here that this focus on a personal connection as my strategic key only worked because I sincerely liked to connect with people and cared about my players. I wanted the parents to know my goal was to develop the whole person.

A strategy has to come from your strengths and your core competencies, and it cannot go against your identity or values.

IS YOUR STRATEGY ALIGNED WITH WHAT YOU DO BEST, OR ARE YOU REACTING TO OTHERS?

I vividly remember a two-game stretch in my first year as a head coach at Morehead State that significantly impacted how

I process the concept of strategy. We played the University of Tennessee-Martin (UT-Martin) early in the season. Young and ambitious, I was preparing like crazy and wanted to give my team as much information about the opponent as I could.

I built an entire game plan around reacting to the plays UT-Martin ran. I tried to cram as much information about the opponent into my players' heads as possible. We were going to be the best-prepared team ever and correctly anticipate UT-Martin's every move.

To say the least, it did not go as planned. I tried to communicate an overwhelming amount of detail to my players in a short period of time. There was just too much for them to process.

With my players worried more about what the other team was doing, we were not playing our game, and it sapped our energy. We were completely listless and took a beating.

The game against UT-Martin was on Thursday night, and we had another game scheduled for Saturday at Eastern Illinois. As was typical in those days, we did not return to our home campus; we just got back on the bus and traveled to the next game.

I remember being in a hotel room and trying to figure out what I should do now. I have been unbelievably blessed with a network of other coaches I could connect with—especially in times of struggle. That network definitely includes Renee Ladner, someone I trusted to bounce ideas off of and get great advice back.

We had previously been assistant coaches together on the staff at Florida, and now she was at Ole Miss. I gave her a call and described the situation as I saw it, asking for her thoughts.

"Matthew, it doesn't matter what you have in your brain," she told me. "It's what the players can absorb into their brains. Stop trying to make it about what the other team can do. For now, just make it about what your team can do."

This was a turning point for me as a head coach. It gave me the insight that a strategy needed to be based on your team or organization's identity, not a reaction to what someone else might be doing. That revelation served me well for my whole career.

It turned out to be pretty good advice in the short run, too.

At the practices leading up to Saturday's game, we did not even talk about Eastern Illinois. We only concerned ourselves with our systems. I used a few simple, core drills to remind us of who we were and what we did.

We came out and beat the stuffing out of Eastern Illinois. We unleashed all our energy, focusing on what we did best, and the results were superb.

To be clear, I am not advocating that you completely forget opponents, competitors, or outside forces when creating a strategy. I have already shared several instances where scouting and planning for specific situations have paid off.

What I am saying is that your strategy should *prioritize* what you do best. It should be primarily about your processes. It can be easy to see what a competitor is doing and want to copy it or spend all your efforts reacting to it. That can be appropriate in some limited situations, but not if you are trying to graft on a strategy that does not fit your organization's DNA.

As you create a strategy, ask:

- What are our core competencies, and how can we use them to create the right strategy?
- Does our strategy benefit from the processes we are best at executing?
- Is the strategy simple enough that I can communicate it to others?

HELP WITH STRATEGY

One thing to notice about the story above is my phone call to Coach Ladner. It can be extremely helpful to have a small handful of people you trust to bounce strategic ideas off of and give you suggestions on strategy.

As an expert at what you do, you can always observe what you see on a calculating, logical level and then create a strategy from it. Sometimes, though, you are trapped in a certain habit of mind that does not allow you to see what needs to be seen. Get out of your own brain. Open up to a trusted colleague or mentor. Tell them honestly what you are facing. Then listen.

However, I do think it is important to limit the number of voices. I always lean toward simplicity over complexity when possible. When it comes to strategy, you should not be treating it as a poll where you are aggregating opinions. You should not be calling everyone you know who might have an idea. You definitely should not be flailing around on Google, searching desperately for strategy answers. Keep it simple by limiting your sources of input.

Another source for strategy ideas is asking, "What strategy can I copy? Who is already doing this well, and how do they do it?"

At first, this advice may seem to contradict the idea that your strategy should play to your core competencies. However, that is only true if you choose to mimic a strategy that does not fit you and your team.

You can still get great ideas from mentors, competitors, and peers. You just need to use the Honesty tool and ask whether this strategy aligns with the talent, resources, and culture of your organization.

SUSTAINABLE STRATEGIES

A business my wife Jenna and I currently co-own is a restaurant in the "fast casual" space called Rise N' Brine Chicken Biscuits.

The plan is to have many locations, but as of now, this potential culinary empire stands at a grand total of one store in Lexington, Kentucky—and that is a 100% intentional decision. Together with our business partners, Matt and Betsy Borland, we looked deeply into this industry and discovered a pattern among fast casual restaurants.

Over and over, the same thing happens: Fast casual restaurants launch a store (or a small handful of stores) and see remarkable sales. Then, they immediately open a bunch more, and sometimes even more soon after that.

In many cases, it turns out they grow too big, too fast, and everything folds up within five years. Fast casual dining is an industry full of meteoric rises, followed by spectacular falls. The strategy of most of these businesses was essentially, "If you have a chance to grow like wildfire, then grow, and do it *now*."

In one way, it sounds like a great strategic guiding principle. After all, what business doesn't love growth?

However, it actually is not a sustainable strategy unless the business has created the right structure and mastered its fundamentals. Growth can magnify problems that were manageable when the company just had one location.

Based on all this, we decided to create a different strategy for Rise N' Brine. Despite a very strong start and healthy numbers, we are intentionally going slow. Our strategy is to focus on our fundamentals, our processes, and our core competencies. We are prioritizing that over fast growth.

This strategy becomes the lens for our decision-making. Without it, we might be tempted to expand based on our results so far; instead, we can pour that energy into continuing to refine our processes, so that if (and when) we expand, the solid foundation is there.

STRATEGIC FLEXIBILITY OR SHORTCUT?

As you think through strategies, it is important to distinguish between a flexible strategy and a shortcut.

I like to think of it this way: A shortcut is violating your principles or going against your core competencies to chase after success, while flexibility is being open to change within the scope of your principles and central processes.

This is admittedly sometimes a distinction that is not always completely straightforward. Occasionally it is clear cut, but other times you need to noodle on it for a while and practice radical honesty to figure it out.

For example, as a basketball coach, I believed in tough, pressure defense. Gritty man-to-man defense was one of our signature strategies. I loved coaching it—and if it were just about what I enjoyed, we would have never taught or played anything but man-to-man.

As my career progressed, however, some of my assistants pushed me to sprinkle in some zone defense for certain limited situations to throw the other team off balance. I was a bit resistant. Was this not exactly what I had counseled against with strategy? I leaned toward always sticking with what we did best.

But I gave it a try and started a small slice of practice on zone. We would still play man-to-man about 90% of the time, but we now had the option to go to it when appropriate to break the other team's rhythm.

What this did was give us the flexibility in our overall strategy to respond to immediate threats. We did not wildly switch from one strategy to another in chasing success. We stayed true to our strategic principles, but added an additional weapon we could use with intentionality.

Compare that to a desperate switching from strategy to strategy any time you do not get the immediate outcome you were hunting. Always looking for that one magical secret or shortcut is not a path to sustained success.

The key is to build the ability to be flexible into your strategies. From a preparation perspective, you have to plan for as many contingencies as is reasonably possible. In practice, we would often spend about two-thirds of the time on our core processes. The rest of the time we would invest in special circumstances.

Let's translate this into a business scenario. Perhaps your marketing team gets most of its best-quality leads from pay-per-click advertising. That is your marketing department's core competency—and to chase other shiny objects that promise a flood of leads would be shortcut thinking.

However, that does not mean you do not build in flexibility to work on other lead sources. It is a matter of setting a strategy that keeps your team focused on what already works great, while intentionally building other lead sources and methods over time. In this scenario, you keep pay-per-click advertising as the priority of your marketing team's efforts, while testing new lead sources as resources allow.

But what happens if even your core processes do not seem to be working? How do you know when a major change of strategy is needed?

THE DISCIPLINE OF EVALUATION

Up to this point, I have advocated strongly sticking with your strategy and not overreacting to every outcome. But there can come a point when a significant change in strategy is called for—at least for some of your goals.

The question is: How do you know when that is? When are you simply switching out of frustration over a few short-term results, and when are you justified in saying, "This just is not working?"

The key is to be disciplined in your evaluation of strategy. The right way to evaluate is *regularly and properly*.

What does that mean, exactly?

"Evaluating properly" is to ground your evaluation in reality—and that means numbers. This is why I strongly encouraged you in the last chapter to attach measurable numbers to your subgoals.

I like to think of proper evaluation as science first, art second. The science is about the numbers and being honest with yourself about what the results reveal about your preparation strategy. Then comes the art, where you ask whether you have given this enough time to bear fruit, or if there are other factors than the strategy at play.

Sometimes, the problem is in the performance of individual team members. Part of your evaluation in this type of situation needs to focus on root causes.

Whenever I would have a player who was not performing well, I would ask myself, "Is this a competency issue or a capability issue?"

If it was a competency issue, that meant they had the ability to do it—they just were not competent at it yet. In this case, that is on the leader. You, as a leader, need to either teach them or challenge them (or both) to get to the standard.

If it is a capability issue, then that needs to be addressed by getting the person into a role they can handle, or parting ways so that they can find where they can better contribute in another organization.

Proper evaluation also means not doing it when you are in an emotional mood after a big setback.

"Evaluating regularly" means you do not shy away from continuous evaluation. Are you backing away from the conflict that evaluation sometimes generates? It can be hard to admit that a strategy is no longer working, or that a key team member is not up to the standard. The disciplined leader does not allow these concerns to stop them from taking an impartial and honest look at what is going on.

"Regularly" also means you have intentionally thought through how big a sample size you need before you decide that a preparation strategy needs to be changed. Sports has this built in, to a certain degree; your winning percentage over the course of a season is a good barometer of a strategy's success or failure.

Sometimes, however, waiting a whole season to make a change can cost you your job. So, using both science (data) and art (experience and intuition), a good coach needs to think hard about what an appropriate timeframe to shift gears is.

A business leader is in the same position. Waiting for annual (or even quarterly) results can lead to big trouble, but overreacting over a couple of poor weeks in a row can also be a bad idea. Leaders who practice the discipline of proper and regular evaluation will discover their mastery of it building over time.

"THE PROBLEM WAS IN HIS OWN LACK OF DISCIPLINE IN FOLLOW-UP AND ACCOUNTABILITY."

Bryan knew his career was stuck in neutral. He had a middle management position with Synergy Solutions, a B2B company renowned for its innovative business services. But Bryan's customer fulfillment team was plagued by inconsistency.

Customer surveys fluctuated wildly, and fulfillment metrics painted a troubling picture: Services were often delayed beyond promised start dates. If you looked at the total customer fulfillment picture, it screamed "mediocrity." Not catastrophic, but far from the excellence Synergy Solutions aspired to, and far from the excellence that could get someone promoted.

Bryan sincerely wanted to do well, and had tried various strategies to improve his team's performance. He experimented with metrics for his direct reports, hoping that data-driven insights would lead to better results. Yet, despite these efforts, nothing seemed to stick. The department's performance remained stubbornly average.

This ate at Bryan. He knew his team had the potential to excel, but nothing was working. One late night, as he reviewed the latest disappointing survey results, a realization struck him: The issue wasn't with the measurements or the team's capabilities. The problem was in his own lack of discipline in follow-up and accountability.

Bryan had always believed in the importance of trust and autonomy. He didn't want to be a micromanager. However, he now saw that his reluctance to consistently follow-up on metrics and confront underperformance was fostering a culture of mediocrity. His team needed more than just metrics; they needed him to hold them accountable.

Determined to turn things around, Bryan devised a plan. First, he committed to regular one-on-one meetings with each team member. These sessions would go beyond discussing numbers; they would delve into the root causes of any issues and set clear, actionable steps for improvement.

He started with Lisa, a project coordinator whose projects were often delayed. In their meeting, Bryan didn't just review her metrics; he asked probing questions to understand her challenges. Lisa revealed that unclear communication from other departments often caused her to face delays. Together, they devised a strategy to improve cross-departmental communication, including setting up brief daily check-ins with key stakeholders.

Next, Bryan tackled the issue of consistent underperformers. He realized that avoiding difficult conversations had only exacerbated the problem. So, he scheduled a candid discussion with Tom, a senior team member whose performance had been lackluster for months. Bryan came up with a coaching plan that would give Tom the chance to improve or move on to something that better suited him.

Bryan also introduced a system of public accountability. In weekly team meetings, they would review key metrics together.

Celebrating successes became a regular part of the agenda, but so did addressing shortcomings openly. This transparency fostered a sense of shared responsibility and encouraged the team to support each other in achieving their goals.

These changes didn't yield immediate miracles, but Bryan gradually began seeing improvements. Customer surveys started to show more consistent satisfaction, and delivery times became more reliable. The team's morale improved as well, as clear goals and strategies for reaching them gave them purpose.

Bryan's disciplined approach to follow-up and accountability transformed the customer fulfillment department. He learned that while autonomy and trust were vital, they needed to be balanced with consistent oversight and support. By actively engaging with his team, addressing issues head-on, and holding everyone accountable, he turned a mediocre department into one known for reliability and excellence.

SEVEN

EXECUTING A DETAILED PREPARATION PLAN

A T KENTUCKY, WE HAD A PRACTICE PLAN EACH DAY that was printed out and posted for all to see. It was important that it be detailed and visible. There could be no question that we had a clear daily plan that was intentionally created with care and thought.

It meant there would be no wasted motion, no wondering what we would do next, and no vague wondering whether we had a purpose in everything we did. I am convinced that this daily habit of having a detailed, written plan was one of the key reasons why we won 70% of our games during my tenure.

The origin of this was something born partly out of necessity. By the time I got my first college head coaching job, I had been an assistant with enough great coaches that I had a pretty good idea of how I would run a practice.

I could have sketched out a rough practice plan to guide myself, or even kept it all in my head. At the time, though, I had some assistant coaches who were relatively young and inexperienced. This was no knock on them. They were a high character, hard working group. However, I felt it would be beneficial for them to have a detailed, written practice plan.

As things evolved, I began to see that a detailed and written preparation plan had great advantages—and not just for newer coaches.

Perhaps you are tempted to nod along with the idea that a plan needs to be written out in detail, but then later decide, "I know what needs done, I do not need to spend time writing it down."

I cannot emphasize enough how important it is to get plans out of your head and down on paper (or a digital document). The benefits are huge.

THE REASONS TO WRITE DOWN YOUR PREPARATION PLAN IN DETAIL

It Makes the Purpose Completely Clear

Clear purpose generates energy. When a team knows exactly what they should be working on, no brain space is used wondering whether they are working on the right things. They can put their full concentration on what is in front of them.

There is also no downtime spent figuring out what is next. Everyone can plainly see the plan and that they are contributing to the organization being *ready to win*.

It Signals You Value Your Team's Time

Great leaders respect their teams. If that respect is genuine, it will be demonstrated in lots of little ways.

When you take the time to create a detailed written plan, it says, "Team, your time is valuable. What you do is important to me and to the organization. I value your work enough that I want it to not be wasted on anything inessential."

These are the messages a detailed, written plan sends.

It Allows Others to Keep the Trains Running In Your Absence

You may truly be an expert, and you might be capable of keeping a detailed plan inside the confines of your brain. However, there may be times when vacation, business travel, illness, or personal situations necessitate an absence—either short or long. Do you really want your team wasting any time when you cannot be there yourself?

Write down your preparation plan and make it detailed!

WHAT SHOULD BE INCLUDED
IN A PREPARATION PLAN?

How do you go about creating an exceptional preparation plan? The foundation of the answer should grow organically out of the previous two chapters. Everything needs to be aligned and motivated by your goals, subgoals, and strategy.

For each task on your preparation plan, you should be able to say exactly how it fits the strategy and gets you closer to a subgoal. Any task that does not fit the strategy and get you closer to the subgoal needs to be eliminated.

Remember also that it will be normal for many of the tasks on the preparation plan to be repetitive.

That definitely applied to our practices. There were certain areas of the game where we wanted to dominate the other team, and the only way to do that was to drill it day after day.

Similarly, every business has core areas that are its lifeblood. How you get more customers probably requires some preparation that is repetitive. The same goes for how you fulfill your promises to your customers. These kinds of core tasks should have a significant place in any detailed preparation plan.

Remember that not every part of a preparation plan needs to be filled with creative wizardry or an attempt to reinvent the wheel.

THE BIG 5 OF A PREPARATION PLAN

Of course, I cannot hand you a preparation plan that fits your particular industry and unique organization. Only your goals and strategies can guide you on the precise details.

However, there are five key areas you can use as a guide to creating a powerhouse preparation plan. Each one is an area for you to reflect on as you create your plan. They are:

- Prioritization
- Timelines
- Responsibility & Accountability
- Resources
- Curiosity

Let's look closer at each of these.

Prioritization

Every business, sports team, and organization would love to be prepared for anything and everything. Obviously, that is not realistic given the fact that there is always limited time and there are only so many resources. This is why the ability to think hard about prioritization is such a key skill for leaders.

The good news is that creating goals, subgoals, and strategies can show you the way forward. When you have clarity on goals and strategies, that will strongly point to which of your tasks have the highest priority.

But even within this framework, you will still have to make some decisions on how to best spend your team's time and resources. The tiebreaker is always: Which of these tasks gets us closer to our goals, and does it faster?

Timelines

As you create a detailed preparation plan, there can be a lot of moving parts. One of the key things to do is isolate time factors and ask whether the time to prepare makes sense.

Look at each task and ask: How long will this likely take? If one task is dependent on others, does the sequence work together to get you to your goal on time?

Keep in mind that you are not just creating a timeline to have something done on time, but done on time and *with quality*.

Responsibility & Accountability

As you add tasks to your preparation plan, look at each one and ask:

- Who will be responsible for this getting done?
- Is there measurable data that can be put on this task?
- How will I communicate these standards to the team?

Without having accountability standards built into your plan, it will be a very weak guiding document.

Resources

This is a big one when putting together a preparation plan. There are two major considerations.

One is not expecting more from your resources (which includes people, technology, finances, and facilities) than they can realistically provide. Do not build a plan on hope or a dream outcome you wish you could have. Build it on what you have.

The other major consideration is almost the flip side of the first. Are you truly looking at all the resources you do have? Are you weighed down by limiting beliefs? Are you limiting your people on past results or can they achieve more? It is possible that your team has more to give and you will bring out untapped potential.

Are you using the technology you *do* have to its capacity? Stay realistic, but do not be afraid to question whether you are maximizing the resources you have at your disposal.

Curiosity

This is a continuation of the idea of thinking through your resources. When you put together a preparation plan, review it as a whole. Where might you be stuck in thought patterns that have you doing the same old mediocre preparation?

Again, there is a balance here. Repetition and systems that get consistent results are definitely a friend of sustained success. That should not stop us from asking more of ourselves with curious questions. Here are just a few examples of the kind of questions that can spur ideas about resources:

- Where were resources lacking in our most recent project? How did that impact the results? (Be as specific as possible)
- What are resources that do not cost money, and are we thinking of them? (Loosen up your thinking here: Even something like the attitude of the team can be a resource)
- Looking at the people on the team, is everyone in a role that fits them? Can we explore with openness and curiosity whether everyone's talents are being used in a way that fits both them and the project?

EVERYTHING YOU HAVE LEARNED UP TO THIS POINT COULD BE WORTHLESS...

Everything in this book you have learned up till now could be worthless. The levels of preparation. The mindsets. The goals, subgoals, strategies, and detailed, written preparation plans. All of it.

Unless you are also ready to execute as a true leader.

As much as I believe in the value of a detailed, written plan, it is just a plan. And plans do not execute—leaders do. What you have created up to this point is a superb roadmap to the destination of sustained success.

But the roadmap is not the actual road. It is your leadership that will make sure the preparation actually happens.

THE THREE WAYS TO LEAD

There are three basic ways to lead, and you need them all if you want to be ready to win.

- Lead with Integrity
- Lead with Education
- Lead with Discipline

These three methods of leadership are not hard concepts to understand, but they can be hard to live out.

When You Lead with Integrity, You Lead by Example

The first way, leadership by Integrity, may be the most important when it comes to setting the tone for a culture of preparation. You reveal your integrity as a leader when you set the right example.

Leading by example has obvious sides and more subtle ones. Pay attention to both.

On the obvious front, you need to be prepared in your own role as leader or people will notice.

Are you often unprepared for meetings? Do you not know basic facts when someone asks you a question you should know the answer to?

I think as leaders, we often excuse ourselves for certain situations where we are unprepared. We are often so busy that it gives us the perfect excuse: We were focused on higher priority items.

Do we stop to consider how we appear to others, though? If we are too busy, we may come across as distracted (or even hypocritical) to those we are leading.

I always told my players I had an open door policy for them. "Whether the President of the University or the President of the United States is in my office, if you come to see me, I will pause what I am doing and hear what you have to say."

I meant it. But as good as it sounded, word got back to me that there had been some grumbling among a few players that I was not in my office a lot in the first place.

Of course, I knew what they did not: My schedule was thoroughly planned out and packed from morning until night. All they saw, however, was a coach who was not always in his office.

I decided I would start sending them a picture of my calendar every morning (this was back before there were apps that let you easily share access to your calendar).

This served a lot of great purposes. For one, if they *did* need to find me, they would see where I was and when they could find me.

More importantly, it showed them I was definitely practicing what I preached. My staff and I always stressed to them the importance of planning out their week on a calendar. Now, they could see that I did the exact same thing.

They could also see that each day, my planner literally went all the way to an entry that said, "Lights Out." My days were fully planned out. Preparation was not something I just talked about; it was a crucial part of my own life that I fully believed in.

Leadership by Integrity can also be more subtle.

I was always a firm believer that exceptional conditioning was a non-negotiable if you wanted to be a winning basketball team. From off-season all the way through season's end, conditioning was always a huge point of emphasis. That was one of the pillars of our identity.

As you might imagine, this was not always the most popular stance. The plain fact is that conditioning is hard. It requires pushing through physical barriers and a level of mental toughness that can be uncomfortable.

So, I made a point of also pushing myself to stay in shape. Of course, I was not going to be on the court, and whether I was in shape or not had no direct impact on our winning or losing. It was also obvious that my conditioning could not (and would not) be to the level of a young athlete.

By pushing myself, I wanted to send the message that I truly did believe in physical conditioning and that I would not ask them to push themselves if I was not willing to do the same.

I wanted them to not just *hear* that I did this; I wanted them to *see* it, too. There was a stair climber machine in our training room, which you could see through a window in our practice facility's hallway. I made sure to use it. The players would get a kick out of seeing me on the stair climber before or after practice, and would knock on the window and laugh at their coach as he sweated and huffed and puffed.

I even told them why I did it: That in my small way, I was with them in dedication to being physically strong. These small messages add up to you becoming a leader people want to follow.

When You Lead with Education, You Teach People to Raise Their Performance

We also need to lead through Education. In the last chapter, I touched on the ideas of competence and capability. Any performance that falls below the standard (in business or sports) can always be categorized as one or the other. It is either a capability problem or a competence problem. If certain standards are not being met during the execution of your preparation plan, it is time to diagnose the root cause.

There is not a lot that can be done if a person is truly incapable of reaching the standard. As previously stated, you need to either find another place for them or they need to move to another organization that better matches their capability.

More often, though, it is a competence issue. Maybe they need someone to help them develop their skills. Or, perhaps no one has ever taken the time to explain what they are doing wrong. It is also possible that up till now, no one has been clear with them on expectations and standards.

Whatever the reason, it is up to the leader to diagnose the issue and find a solution. This is where teaching comes in. A good question to ask frequently is: By what means can you educate your team members to get them to raise their competency level?

When You Lead With Discipline, You Create Accountability

It has already been noted that measurables have to be part of goals, strategies, and preparation plans. By themselves, though, those are just numbers on a piece of paper or spreadsheet.

There need to be real world consequences when the standards in the plan are not met. Naturally, the severity will depend on the situation, but at a minimum, there has to be a commitment to calling it out when the team comes up short of the mark.

Leading by Discipline also means being willing to call out problems on the spot—not just in retrospect. Of course, this kind of calling out needs to be done without humiliating a person or being destructive in your criticism.

Many leaders fail to make a correction in the moment through either fear or inattention. If you want an accountable team, immediate feedback is a crucial part of it.

Monitor how your team is executing on the preparation plan and how they are doing reaching the subgoals. When you observe an action that contradicts what you are trying to accomplish, constructively break it down with the individual or team right away.

THIS KIND OF LEADERSHIP HAS A CUMULATIVE IMPACT

When you combine the three ways of leadership, you are creating a team culture. Your team sees a leader who creates purpose, reflects with thoughtful intention, and is willing to work hard to the same standard as everyone else.

Do this consistently day after day, and there will be a cumulative effect. Everyone gets used to being a team that is powerfully positioned to win, and that drives a culture where sustained success is simply the expectation. Once you reach that level, the results begin to grow exponentially.

The key to this cumulative power is a continuous commitment to showing up as a leader every day. Talk and inspiration may give a brief boost, but eventually, your people see behind the curtain.

"IT WAS MORE OF A WISH THAN A CONCRETE PLAN."

Kelly is only a few years out of college and has always been passionate about numbers and the world of finance. Working at SportsVision Marketing, a well-known sports marketing firm, she dreamed of earning a leadership position in the finance department.

Initially, it was more of a wish than a concrete plan. Kelly eventually had to acknowledge this hard truth to herself and admit that wishing wasn't going to get it done. Kelly decided to get serious about her ambitions. One weekend, she sat down and crafted a detailed action plan.

She listed out the skills she needed to develop, the relationships she needed to build, and the milestones she needed to achieve. Her plan included both short- and long-term goals, breaking them down into manageable steps.

With her action plan in hand, Kelly transformed her approach to each day. She started using a daily planner, meticulously mapping out all her activities and ensuring they aligned with her overarching goal of earning a leadership position. She would spend fifteen minutes every morning filling out her planner, detailing her tasks for the day and reflecting on her progress.

To build her skills, Kelly enrolled in advanced finance and management courses online. She dedicated an hour each evening to studying, enhancing her knowledge of financial analysis, strategic planning, and leadership. On weekends, she attended workshops and webinars relevant to her industry, always seeking to learn from experts and stay ahead of trends.

Networking became another key focus for Kelly. She made it a point to attend company events, engage in conversations with colleagues from different departments, and seek out mentorship opportunities. She reached out to senior leaders within SportsVision Marketing to ask for their advice and feedback on her career aspirations. These interactions not only expanded her network but also provided valuable insights into what it took to succeed in a leadership role.

Kelly also took initiative in her current role, volunteering for challenging projects that required collaboration with other departments and consistently going above and beyond her regular duties, taking on additional responsibilities that showcased her commitment and potential as a future leader.

One of the most significant changes Kelly made was seeking regular feedback. She scheduled monthly check-ins with her manager to discuss her progress and areas for improvement. These conversations were invaluable, providing Kelly with a clear understanding of what she needed to focus on and how she was perceived within the company.

Kelly recognized in retrospect that writing down her plan was vital. It had caused a profound shift in clarifying her purpose and connecting it to action. No longer was she aimlessly wishing for a promotion; she was actively working toward it, tracking her progress and adjusting her strategies as needed. Each day, as she reviewed her planner, she could see the steps she had taken and the milestones she had reached. This sense of direction and accomplishment fueled her motivation and reinforced her belief in her ability to achieve her goal.

Months of dedication and strategic effort paid off. During her annual performance review, Kelly's manager commended her for her exceptional growth and proactive approach. She was informed that a leadership position would be opening up in the finance department, and Kelly was encouraged to apply.

SYSTEMIZATION

HAVE TO LAUGH A LITTLE WHEN I THINK BACK TO 2005, when I first got hired at Morehead State. At that point, I had only been in coaching for 10 years—and that included high school.

Sure, I had been around many great coaches by then. And yes, I had put in a lot of hard work to understand the game as deeply as I could and develop my coaching skills.

But remembering it now, two things stick out. The first is that I was *so* excited to be a college head coach. I mean, I was over the moon excited and ready to take on the world. The second is how unaware I was of all the things I did not know. That's the part that makes me look back at my younger self and laugh a little.

Many fans on the outside looking in would always say to me as a head coach that it must be the coolest job in the world.

What I didn't know at first (and what people outside of it don't, either) is that the complexity and pressure of leading an NCAA basketball team is more than you would think. Sometimes—a lot of the time—cool is the last thing you are feeling.

Don't misunderstand, I am certainly not complaining. As high-level college coaches, we are very well-compensated and there are many satisfactions to the work, despite the long hours.

My point is simply that inexperienced leaders are often in for a surprise as they rise through the ranks by the complexity and newness of many of their challenges. That certainly happened to me at Morehead State, and then all over again at Kentucky.

There were absolutely days when I was just treading water. I was sincerely committed to the Winning Tools at Morehead State, but I had just come up with them—and if I am honest with myself, back then, they were more of an inspirational slogan. They had not yet turned into a fully developed leadership system.

When you get into these new, more complex situations, what hits you full force is that the most successful leaders cannot fly by the seat of their pants. You recognize that you have to lift your preparation game or else you will fail. Raising your game takes more than goals, strategies, and detailed preparation plans.

You also need systems. Great leaders are great systemizers. Why are systems so important?

- If you constantly had to create detailed preparation plans from scratch for every goal, that would be too much to manage. Systems become organizational habits that get crucial tasks and preparation done, without having to rethink it every time.

- Systems also allow you to have a firm foundation of core processes you can trust. This in turn can make you more willing to branch out and investigate ways to keep improving. Once you have the fundamentals covered by a system, you feel more confident in exploring the edges.

- Systems keep you aware of what needs to happen, while avoiding the energy drain of micromanagement.

So, if systems are so great, why do many leaders struggle to establish them?

In my experience, there are two blocks to instituting systems. One is the "fighting fires" mentality that never takes a step back to categorize the issues that are flying at them. Everything is handled as if it is a brand new problem to be dealt with ad hoc. In this way, the leader can never find the time or principles to build a system.

The other block I have witnessed is expecting the wrong things from a system. Some leaders want to carve a system in stone. Then, they hope to kick back and enjoy themselves while the system does the leading for them.

In my experience, it doesn't work that way. Systems are not for relieving you of the responsibility of leadership. Systems are there to provide good habits and routines and increase efficiency. They are not self-perpetuating like some kind of magical machine. The leader is there to consistently engage and evaluate the system.

A solid system will facilitate evaluation without deteriorating into micromanagement.

THE DIFFERENCE BETWEEN SYSTEMS AND MICROMANAGING

In some minds, systems sound like a constraint on freedom and creativity. But a good system is not about stifling people or controlling their thoughts and actions. It is about giving them the structure to do their best work.

As I mentioned earlier, I had a system at Kentucky where my assistants handled the scouting duties on a rotating basis. The way it worked was that each assistant would scout every third game. They knew the general expectations for the report, and they knew the deadline for completing it.

Past that, I let them manage the process how they saw fit. I did not tell them how to do it. I did not tell them when to do it. If they wanted to get up early and complete it, fine. If they wanted to pull an all-nighter, fine.

My concern as a leader within this system was quality control. The system only works if the leader evaluates the quality of the work regularly. In this case, that was a scouting report, and my assistants knew I would be looking for something more than a "here is my finished work product" attitude.

The system was there to free me from micromanaging their process. It was up to them to get it done right and get it done on time. Giving them room granted them the freedom to develop and freed me up from constantly looking over their shoulder.

However, this system only works if I also serve as an evaluator of what they accomplished. That is what ensures the system is not cranking out mediocre widgets that do not move you closer to the goal of winning.

It is important to note that this does not mean a leader should never get involved in a team member's process. In this example, if I had an assistant consistently doing a mediocre scouting report, it would have been appropriate for me to ask about the process they were using.

This could be an opportunity to help them grow in their knowledge and planning of their own preparation. When you have these opportunities as a leader, the message should be twofold. One half is to challenge them to get better (and be honest that they need to). The other half is that you care about their development, and there is a better way that can help them grow.

I should also add that there will be some systems where it is more appropriate to direct how an individual carries out a task. For example, many companies want individual salespeople to follow a set process with a prospect.

How detailed your system is will be dictated by the circumstances and what you want to accomplish.

CREATING YOUR SYSTEM

To some degree, systems will grow organically out of your detailed preparation plans. For anything that is a core part of your business, you will find yourself repeating the same preparation plans again and again.

Hopefully, you are refining the plan where appropriate—and of course, constantly evaluating it. At a certain point, it makes sense to institute it as a full-blown system for your team.

There is another way to go about system building which can complement the above approach. I call this method ICE, which stands for "Identify-Commit-Evaluate."

When I consult with businesses, one thing I often discover is that the leaders and their teams do not know who they are.

They have not made intentional decisions on the fundamentals that will guide them when making day-to-day decisions in the business. Naturally, you know by now that for me, the fundamental identity is the Winning Tools.

My first priority is radical honesty. My second is hard work. My third is discipline. And I know these all complement each other and work together as a powerful identity.

This is my blueprint for how I am going to live, and this is the basis of my leadership when guiding others. It is what I am going to fall back on in a crisis, and it is what I am going to maintain during great times.

While I recommend the Winning Tools as a great identity that anyone can adopt, you may already have your own set of guiding principles. Or, you may want to forge your own.

That, of course, is a decision only you can make. However, you cannot make forward progress toward sustained success until you clearly define an identity.

Once you have your principles spelled out, it is time to commit. Can you and your team honestly say, "*Yes*, this is who we want to be, and this identity will power us in both success and adversity?" If you can affirm that, then commit to it.

Lastly, you need to evaluate. Are you living up to the identity as a leader? Is your team upholding these principles? A true leader will want to look at *all* the information. Don't only seek out confirmations of your own biases. Do not just look for good, affirming data. Take it all in: The good, the bad, and the ugly.

Once you are comfortable that you have the right identity and can live it out, it is time to ask what core systems you can build which align with that identity.

SUMMARIZING THE IDEAL SYSTEM

At a high level, here are the main points a good system should have:

- Clear expectations on what needs to be accomplished, and to what standard. Check these fundamental expectations to make sure they align with your identity.
- A timeframe for accomplishing those expectations.
- Regular evaluation points for quality control. Teach and hold to account where appropriate.
- Regular evaluation to determine whether the system is keeping you on track to meet your goals and win more often.

Check every system you create against these four points, because these are the defining characteristics of a good system.

Reader Bonus: Go to *coachmatthewmitchell.com/ resources* and download the System Filter worksheet to help you create a system that makes sense for your organization.

BEND, BUT DON'T BREAK

In golf, there is a seemingly endless variety of advice on every topic. Your head can spin bouncing from one seemingly surefire tip to another. But there is one piece of advice that is almost universal: Create a pre-shot routine and stick with it.

A steady routine gets you in the right mindset for a consistent swing. In general, this is great advice—but should you *always* do it?

It reminds me of a story from the great golf coach, Hank Haney. I love golf and had the thrill of taking a lesson from Hank (and I always wish I could replicate the swing I had during that lesson when my game goes sideways!).

Haney coached Tiger Woods for six years when Woods was at the absolute top of his game. In 2006, Woods was playing in the Open Championship at the Royal Liverpool Golf Club at Hoylake, and he was particularly amazing in that tournament. Nick Faldo afterward described Woods' ball-striking as "sheer perfection," and he was far from alone in his praise.

Haney particularly remembered that on the 18th hole of the final day, Woods had a shot to seal his win. The 18th hole on that course has a tight out of bounds on both the left and right. With a championship almost in hand, you want to avoid a big mistake.

In this scenario, if we go back to the standard golf advice to never vary your pre-shot routine, Woods should do exactly what he always does. But Woods, the best golfer on the planet at the time, did something different.

Haney said he took about 10 practice swings before the shot, many more than his normal amount. Haney attributed this to Woods being nervous. "There isn't anybody who plays any sport that doesn't get in a situation where they're nervous."

But the difference with Woods was this: "When Tiger Woods would get nervous, he would deepen his commitment to what he was doing," Haney said. He slowed himself down at a key moment, and it worked. Woods finished off the hole to win his third Claret Jug and 11th professional major.

What this says to me is that Tiger Woods had a system (his pre-shot routine), but also the mental flexibility to vary it. He slowed himself down to match the situation.

Routines and systems give you the confidence to be flexible when your leadership instincts tell you that you need to deviate. Flexibility is the ability to bend, knowing you will snap back into form.

The system is the form. It is easier to take that risk when you are confident you and your team can snap right back to the proven system.

This can come in handy as a leader. In January 2020, Kentucky had two very difficult games to kick off our SEC conference schedule. We opened on the road against South Carolina on a Thursday. They were the favorites to win the national championship.

We got our doors blown off, and it was never close. We were down by double digits the whole game. Still, I stayed positive with my team during the game. Even immediately after, I told them to shake it off and move on. It was "just one of those nights."

Then I watched the film on the plane ride home. As I broke the game down, I could see this was less about how good South Carolina was, and more about how we had not put in a good effort. As it turned out, this was not just one of those nights where nothing bounced our way. We fully deserved to get blown out.

It wasn't going to get any easier, either. We had another tough game coming up just a couple of days later on Sunday. Tennessee was coming to Kentucky, and that meant we had a good chance of starting 0–2.

The standard wisdom on short rest between games is not to overwork your players at practice. Your team is already worn out from the Thursday game. If you push them too hard at practice, the tank will be empty on Sunday.

But I had an intuition that what my team needed was a message about working hard. Otherwise, I sensed we would be dealing with a chronic lack of effort all season. I was willing to risk a tired group versus Tennessee to get the message across.

So work we did. In fact, my one-time boss at Florida, Carolyn Peck, came to the three practices we had leading up to the Tennessee game. She was doing prep work because she would be one of the television commentators for the game, which was going to be televised on ESPN. Early in the broadcast, Carolyn said she didn't know if Kentucky would have anything in the tank to play this game. The practices were the most physically demanding she had seen!

As it turned out, nobody needed to worry about Kentucky's fatigue. We came out and controlled the entire game from the opening tip. It was a tremendous performance, and our season was back on track.

What I had done was a big departure from the norm. But by then, I had been at Kentucky for more than a decade, and I trusted our system. I trusted that even if we started 0–2, we could find our way back. To not have maximum effort practices after the lackadaisical performance against South Carolina would have violated our identity priority of Hard Work.

This is why systems are so valuable for allowing the freedom of risk taking. They are like a rock solid base you can return to if your experiment goes wrong. If it goes right, you have another tool in the toolbox.

READY TO WIN

It is time to put this all together. You know the levels of preparation, the mindsets, the goals, subgoals, strategies, and systems. I now want to leave you with a solid plan for taking action.

"THE COMPANY IS NOT LIVING UP TO ITS OWN NAME."

Carlos is the CEO of Peak Performance Enterprises, and lately he has been thinking the company is not living up to its own name.

The organization provides consultant services that help other businesses achieve peak performance. Carlos knows his own company is good at what it does, but honesty makes him admit that they do not have the systems in place to truly drive peak performance.

Carlos has never been one to hold back, so he dives right in.

First, he decided to define clear expectations for his team. For example, Carlos laid out specific goals for each department. For the marketing team, it was not just a vague goal of increasing social media engagement, but a specific objective of achieving a 20% rise in conversion rates. For the sales team, it was getting laser-focused on reaching quarterly targets consistently, without compromising on customer satisfaction. Each facet of the business was given a specific objective.

Next, Carlos established a timeframe for accomplishing these expectations. He introduced a quarterly planning cycle, breaking the annual goals down into manageable three-month segments. Each quarter would have specific milestones, allowing teams to focus on short-term achievements that collectively contributed to the long-term vision. He emphasized the importance of deadlines, making it clear that meeting these timeframes was non-negotiable.

To ensure quality control, Carlos implemented regular evaluation points. Every month, each department would submit a detailed progress report highlighting achievements, challenges, and areas needing improvement. Carlos also scheduled bi-weekly meetings with department heads to review these reports and provide feedback. "This isn't about micromanaging," he explained. "It's about ensuring we maintain our standards and continuously improve."

Finally, Carlos introduced a new role within the company—a Quality Assurance Manager—whose sole responsibility was to audit processes and outcomes. This role was crucial in identifying gaps and making sure every project met the company's high standards.

Through all these specific actions, Carlos was able to pinpoint what was working and what wasn't. If a strategy failed to produce the desired results, it was re-evaluated and modified. This adaptability ensured Peak Performance remained agile and responsive to both internal and external changes.

Implementing systems transformed Peak Performance Enterprises. Clear expectations, well-defined timeframes, regular quality checks, and continuous evaluations created a culture of accountability and excellence. The employees felt more focused and driven, knowing exactly what was expected of them and how their work contributed to achieving peak performance.

BRINGING IT ALL TOGETHER WITH THE PREPARATION ACTIVATOR

OES THIS SOUND FAMILIAR?

We read a book. We get excited about some of what it can do for us. And then we close the book and forget most of what we've learned.

I don't want that to happen here.

I want you to finish this book strong. I want you to get "hands on" and see and feel the power of preparation when it is done well.

I have created The Preparation Activator, a seven-day jump-start to help these concepts soak into your brain. To state the obvious, you will not be an expert after seven days. However, if you follow it faithfully, you will begin the formation of habits that I know will resonate with you and create some positive internal feedback. As the name implies, it is intended to activate you on the path of preparation!

If you take it seriously, you will begin down a path that can change your life.

WHAT YOU'LL NEED

Get a blank notebook that is dedicated exclusively to the exercises below. I'll refer to this from here on out as your *Ready to Win Journal* (RTWJ). I hope that even after the seven days, you will continue using the journal as a place to reflect on preparation and leadership.

Reader Bonus: Go to *coachmatthewmitchell.com/resources* and download the *Ready to Win Journal*. It contains easy-to-use worksheets to help you implement the Preparation Activator.

THE 7-DAY PREPARATION ACTIVATOR

Day 1

Give Chapter 1 a quick review. Specifically, review the five levels of preparation (Casual, Cursory, Compliant, Committed, and Constant). Grab your RTWJ and create an entry to assess which category describes your preparation behavior (use the Honesty tool!).

If you are currently at the Casual, Cursory, or Compliant level, reflect next on whether you can sincerely vow to live at the Commitment level of preparation. As you continue your journal entry, think about the potential roadblocks to raising your level. Also reflect on the rewards you might expect when you commit.

Finally, end the journal entry with a written promise to live at the Commitment level of preparation. Or, if you are not ready for that, then promise to return to the journal and reflect on what is holding you back from making this commitment.

Note: See the "Preparation Reflection" in the *Ready to Win Journal,* available for download at *coachmatthew mitchell.com/resources.*

Day 2

It is morning and you are grabbing your RTWJ again.

This morning, you are starting a habit that you will do every day from now on.

Answer specifically for today. Tomorrow, you will do these same three exercises. And the day after that. And the day after that. Keep rinsing and repeating forever, and watch your life satisfaction and success skyrocket.

3 Mindsets in 3 Minutes

Get up early and go to a quiet place.

In the 1st Minute, recognize one good thing you did yesterday. Maybe it was the worst day ever, but you can still pull out one thing. If it is work- or career-related, great. But it can also be as simple as, "I gave my kid a hug yesterday."

Notice that recognizing something good is not about lying or being a Pollyanna. Maybe you *did* have a bad day. You are not saying, "Everything was sunshine and roses yesterday." You are simply acknowledging that even on the worst of days, you can pull out a small piece of success.

This shifts your focus in the right direction and gives you more energy to find ways to get more of those wins today.

And if you had a great day, even better. Pick out the biggest win and reflect on it.

Committing to this small exercise every day builds into your thought world that every single day, you had success. Do it enough days, and you'll begin to believe that you are truly a person of sustained success—and I promise you some of the wins will get bigger and bigger.

In the 2nd Minute, think about the biggest, baddest task on your agenda today. What do you feel pressure about that you want to turn away from? How long do you anticipate it taking? (If this is something that is part of a larger project, then just think about how long you need to work on it today.) Look at your schedule. Figure out the earliest possible slot you can fit it in. Then commit to knocking it out using the following formula: Today from [specific time] to [specific time], I will accomplish [specific task].

Then do it.

If you slip up or something truly extraordinary forces you to miss carrying this out, forgive yourself and commit to doing this same exercise tomorrow morning. The one thing you do not want to let slip is doing this simple exercise every morning. Breaking your promises will force you to confront yourself again and again.

By doing this exercise every single day, you will be training yourself to choose each day: Do I want to be a person who inhabits a world of excellence or not? Every time you fulfill your promise to accomplish a challenging task at a specific time, you are building that muscle that truly believes Excellence is Its Own Reward.

Please note that this can even be done on vacation.

"Today at 1:00pm, I will spend a full hour with no distractions being fully present with my daughter."

Or, "This evening at 6:00pm, I will take my spouse out to dinner and focus on only being positive and not complaining about anything."

Do it every day!

For the 3rd Minute, you are going to ask how you can fuel your tank today.

What is going to motivate you today? What past experiences can you recall that can get you excited for today?

> **Note:** For this exercise, use the "3 Habits in 3 Minutes" guide in the *Ready to Win Journal*, available for download at *coachmatthewmitchell.com/resources*.

Day 3

You have your RTWJ in hand again.

Start with the three mindset exercises you did for the first time yesterday. Do them again, asking the same questions but giving today's fresh answers.

Now you are going to add a review of your day's priorities in relation to your calendar. Take at least 10 minutes to do this, and more if necessary (on super-busy or important days, I will sometimes spend an hour planning my priorities).

Do not focus only on work priorities. Do not forget to build spiritual, physical, emotional, and mental health activities and other boosts into your day.

Make notes in your journal about where you will need to be most present. Also, jot down any areas where you need to do some more preparation. When appropriate and possible, make changes to your calendar based on your reflections on priorities.

> **Note**: See "Today's Priorities" in the *Ready to Win Journal,* available for download at *coachmatthewmitchell.com/ resources.*

Day 4

Break out your RTWJ. Repeat the mindset exercises from Day 2 and your review of your day's priorities from Day 3. (Hint: You should be repeating these exercises every day from now until... forever!)

Now return to the end of Chapter 5, where you will find an exercise on formulating subgoals. Try that exercise again today (or for the first time, if you have never done it before). Get in the habit of breaking goals down into manageable milestones.

> **Note**: See the "Subgoal Matching" page in the *Ready to Win Journal,* available for download at *coachmatthe wmitchell.com/resources.*

Day 5

You have your RTWJ. Time to start with the mindset exercises and the day's priorities.

Here is the additional exercise to do today.

Think of your most important upcoming meeting, presentation, or some other huge work challenge. Make a list of three-to-five things you could do to be better prepared for it. Then order them by priority.

Finally, for the top two priorities, brainstorm some strategies you could use to make them happen. Circle your favorite strategy.

> **Note**: See the "Preparation Optimization" page in the *Ready to Win Journal,* available for download at *coach matthewmitchell.com/resources.*

Day 6

Start off with the mindset exercises and the day's priorities in your RTWJ.

Now build off of yesterday's work. You ended by circling your favorite strategy. Next, start a list of tasks that align with the strategy and the subgoal you want to accomplish. Prioritize those tasks and put measurables next to them. If other team members are involved, who would be responsible for each?

The idea of this is that you are growing the kernel of a detailed, written preparation plan.

> **Note**: See the "Strategy Details" page in the *Ready to Win Journal,* available for download at *coachmatthew mitchell.com/resources.*

Day 7

You know the drill by now. Get your RTWJ, do the mindset exercises, and go through the day's priorities.

Today, you are going to reflect on Leadership by Integrity, Leadership by Education, and Leadership by Discipline.

For each of these three areas, write down one thing you could be doing better. It could be something big or something small. When you hit on something you can do, copy that idea from your journal into a slot on your calendar for the upcoming week. Then do it!

> **Note:** See the "Leadership Development" page in the *Ready to Win Journal,* available for download at *coach matthewmitchell.com/resources.*

Day Forever

What might happen in your life if you just kept going? If you did the mindset exercises and priorities every day?

And then what if you took another few minutes to repeat one of the other exercises above? Or turned this journal into a spot to reflect on preparation and leadership as you learn lessons along the way?

It would be transformative. You would be Ready to Win.

BONUS EXERCISE

I would like to share one more exercise with you that is so powerful. I hope you use it as a blueprint for leading a life of character, success, and satisfaction.

The Winning Tools Exercise

As anyone who read my first book knows, I truly believe in and live by The Winning Tools. Not perfectly every day, but it is my blueprint, and it forms the foundation for what I share with others.

Every morning, ask yourself about each of the Winning Tools:

- **What do I need to be honest about today?** This can be something you have been hiding from, a problem you have not quite figured out yet and need to get more clarity on, or something else. Ask this simple question, and the answers for what you need to be honest about will come.

- **What do I need to apply hard work to today?** What are the priorities for your day, and which ones will require the most "elbow grease?" How can you best confront and overcome something you feel lazy about today?

- **What is going to require the most discipline from me today?** We sometimes need to reflect on those tasks that will require the most effort, or make us feel the most anxious or pressured. We need to acknowledge that this will call on us to draw from our reservoir of discipline.

The simple habit of reflecting on each of these categories every day will remind you of who you are and what you believe. Your actions will align with who you want to be.

> **Note:** See the "How will I use the Winning Tools today?" page in the *Ready to Win Journal,* available for download at *coachmatthewmitchell.com/resources.*

CONCLUSION

This book began with a quote by Michael Jordan, and I now want to end it with one, too. He once said: "Some people want it to happen, some wish it would happen, others make it happen."

This perfectly encapsulates something I encourage you to reflect on as you become a person of constant preparation: Everybody wants to win. We sometimes get trapped into thinking we are special just by the fact that we desire great success or dream big. The truth, however, is that wanting it and wishing it do not make you unique.

What *will* make you stand out and win more often is taking action. Your honesty, hard work, and discipline will make the difference. Your preparation and your commitment to sustained success will turn dreams into reality.

Everybody wants to win. But are you Ready to Win? Go make it happen. Then congratulate yourself for investing in your personal development and growth. Sustained success will be *yours*!

Printed in the USA
CPSIA information can be obtained
at www.ICGtesting.com
LVHW092013021124
795368LV00002B/2/J